The Authentic World of Sherlock Holmes

An Evocative Tour of Conan Doyle's Victorian London by Charles Viney

Jeremy Brett as Sherlock Holmes in a still from Granada Television's The Sign of Four. *He is seen on Westminster Bridge.*

The Authentic World of

Sherlock Holmes

An Evocative Tour of Conan Doyle's Victorian London by Charles Viney

Bramley Books

This book is dedicated to
a kind gentleman and Sherlock Holmes enthusiast,
my grandfather Oscar Viney
(1886–1976)

4646 The Authentic World of Sherlock Holmes

This edition published in 1999 by Bramley Books,
Godalming Business Centre,
Woolsack Way, Godalming,
Surrey GU7 1XW

© 1995 Quadrillion Publishing Ltd,
Godalming, Surrey, GU7 1XW

Printed and bound in Italy

ISBN 1-84100-302-6

Contents

Named after William Baker who laid it out from 1755, Baker Street was little changed when Holmes and Watson moved there.

Introduction

Sir Arthur Conan Doyle's masterly evocation of London in the Sherlock Holmes stories has probably done more to form our vision of the late nineteenth century metropolis than any other writer. His portrait of a huge, fog-bound, romantic and sinister city at the apogee of its imperial greatness remains, to this day, extremely convincing and atmospheric. With the great detective operating from his base at 221b Baker Street, and with virtually all the stories and novels set, or partially set, in London, one is drawn to the conclusion that the Sherlock Holmes stories are, essentially, London stories.

Holmes and Watson ranged far and wide across London, a city which, despite the ravages of the Blitz and insensitive urban redevelopment in the post-war years, is easily recognisable to us today. When studying thousands of photographs of late Victorian London as I compiled this book, the city revealed itself to have been both improbably grand and squalid, harbouring great extremes of wealth and poverty – extremes which are still uncomfortably present nearly a century later.

Baring-Gould's *Annotated Sherlock Holmes* (Murray, 1968), the bible for anyone studying this subject, cites 1874 as the earliest known date for a story (The "Gloria Scott"), and 1914 as the latest ('His Last Bow'). Consequently I have, in nearly all cases, reproduced photographs of the London locations mentioned in the Holmes canon between these two dates, and, if possible, tied them even more closely to the date of a story, if known. As a result I have endeavoured to present Holmes's world as he would have known it. For ease of reference the book has been arranged according to the sequence of stories in *The Complete Adventures of Sherlock Holmes*, the most popular omnibus published on both sides of the Atlantic. In addition, each location photographed in this book is referenced against Victorian street maps of London, published in 1888.

Conan Doyle was usually very specific in his London addresses and locations, only changing the name of a street or inserting a false house number if a dire criminal act had been perpetrated on the premises. In most cases the changes are cosmetic. For instance when a murder is committed at '13, Caulfield Gardens' in 'The Adventure of the Bruce-Partington Plans', and the body of the unfortunate Cadogan West is lowered onto the roof of a stationary underground train at the back of the house, I have employed a little detective work of my own to deduce that the fictitious 'Caulfield Gardens' is in fact Cornwall Gardens, Kensington; Circle Line trains are obliged to stop here at the overground intersection with the District Line to this day. On the rare occasions when a completely fictional address or institution is employed, unlisted in Victorian maps of London or *Kelly's Post Office Directories* (1874–1914), and bearing no relation to a street or business in the vicinity, I have omitted it.

Of the fifty-six short stories I have excised only six – 'The Adventure of the Copper Beeches', 'The Crooked Man', 'The Reigate Puzzle', 'The Adventure of the Three Students', 'The Adventure of the Devil's Foot' and 'The Adventure of the Lion's Mane', which are set almost entirely outside London, and contain only passing references to the metropolis. Three of the four novels, *A Study in Scarlet, The Sign of Four* and *The Hound of the Baskervilles*, are extensively set in London and are featured accordingly. I have, however, decided to omit *The Valley of Fear*, which is largely set in Sussex and America, and contains few references to London locations, all of which are featured elsewhere in the book.

Essentially *Sherlock Holmes in London* is a photographic book, and I am indebted to the many skilled, but unknown, Victorian photographers whose work is recorded. Finally, this book would be incomplete without paying homage to Conan Doyle, whose brilliant writing and characterisation have ensured immortality for his creation Sherlock Holmes.

CHARLES VINEY. London, August, 1988.

A Study in Scarlet

Mr. Sherlock Holmes
The Lauriston Garden Mystery ∘ Light in the Darkness
A Continuation of the Reminiscences of John Watson, M.D.,
The Conclusion

Choosing the latter alternative, I began by making up my mind to leave the hotel, and take up my quarters in some less pretentious and less expensive domicile.

Left *The University of London in 1890, when it was located in Burlington Gardens. Designed by James Pennethorne in 1866, the building now houses the Museum of Mankind, the University having vacated the premises earlier this century for its current location in Bloomsbury. (Map 3, M 18)*

Below *The Strand in 1895. The church is St. Mary-le-Strand, designed by James Gibbs and completed in 1717. (Map 3, M 20)*

In the year 1878 I took my degree of Doctor of Medicine of the University of London, and proceeded to Netley to go through the course prescribed for surgeons in the Army. Having completed my studies there I was duly attached to the Fifth Northumberland Fusiliers as assistant surgeon.

I had neither kith nor kin in England, and was therefore as free as air—or as free as an income of eleven shillings and sixpence a day will permit a man to be. Under such circumstances I naturally gravitated to London, that great cesspool into which all the loungers and idlers of the Empire are irresistibly drained. There I stayed for some time at a private hotel in the Strand, leading a comfortless, meaningless existence, and spending such money as I had, considerably more freely than I ought. So alarming did the state of my finances become, that I soon realized that I must either leave the metropolis and rusticate somewhere in the country, or that I must make a complete alteration in my style of living.

On the very day that I had come to this conclusion, I was standing at the Criterion Bar, when someone tapped me on the shoulder, and turning round I recognized young Stamford, who had been a dresser under me at Bart's. The sight of a friendly face in the great wilderness of London is a pleasant thing indeed to a lonely man. In old days Stamford had never been a particular crony of mine, but now I hailed him with enthusiasm, and he, in his turn, appeared to be delighted to see me. In the exuberance of my joy, I asked him to lunch with me at the Holborn, and we started off together in a hansom.

"Whatever have you been doing with yourself, Watson?" he asked in undisguised wonder, as we rattled through the crowded London streets. "You are as thin as a lath and as brown as a nut."

Left Piccadilly Circus in the 1890s. The Criterion Bar can be seen in the right of this photograph and its interior above. Completed in 1874, it was noted for its fine neo-Byzantine ceiling. The Criterion has recently been restored to its former glory. (Map 3, M 19)

Right The Holborn in 1900. Opened as a restaurant in 1874 and extended and redecorated in 1896, it housed a 'Grand Restaurant', private dining rooms, three Masonic temples and a further 14 smaller restaurants. It was demolished in 1955. (Map 3, L 20)

As he spoke, we turned down a narrow lane and passed through a small side-door, which opened into a wing of the great hospital. It was familiar ground to me, and I needed no guiding as we ascended the bleak stone staircase and made our way down the long corridor with its vista of whitewashed wall and dun-coloured doors. Near the farther end a low arched passage branched away from it and led to the chemical laboratory.

This was a lofty chamber, lined and littered with countless bottles. Broad, low tables were scattered about, which bristled with retorts, test-tubes, and little Bunsen lamps, with their blue flickering flames. There was only one student in the room, who was bending over a distant table absorbed in his work. At the sound of our steps he glanced round and sprang to his feet with a cry of pleasure. "I've found it! I've found it," he shouted to my companion, running towards us with a test-tube in his hand. "I have found a re-agent which is precipitated by hæmoglobin, and by nothing else." Had he discovered a gold mine, greater delight could not have shone upon his features.

Above *St. Bartholomew's Hospital (Barts) c. 1900. The 'narrow lane' described by Dr. Watson can be seen to the right of the Pathological Department buildings. (Map 3, L 22)*

Left *Barts Chemical Laboratory, photographed in 1906.*

Right *The American Exchange, Strand, seen in the right of this photograph, taken in 1895, was situated directly in front of the Charing Cross Hotel and station. (Map 3, M 20)*

"We have it all here," said Gregson, pointing to a litter of objects upon one of the bottom steps of the stairs. "A gold watch, No. 97163, by Barraud, of London. Gold Albert chain, very heavy and solid. Gold ring, with masonic device. Gold pin—bull-dog's head, with rubies as eyes. Russian leather cardcase, with cards of Enoch J. Drebber of Cleveland, corresponding with the E. J. D. upon the linen. No purse, but loose money to the extent of seven pounds thirteen. Pocket edition of Boccaccio's 'Decameron,' with name of Joseph Stangerson upon the flyleaf. Two letters—one addressed to E. J. Drebber and one to Joseph Stangerson."

"At what address?"

"American Exchange, Strand—to be left till called for. They are both from the Guion Steamship Company, and refer to the sailing of their boats from Liverpool. It is clear that this unfortunate man was about to return to New York."

For a second or two we might have been a group of statues. Then with an inarticulate roar of fury, the prisoner wrenched himself free from Holmes's grasp, and hurled himself through the window. Woodwork and glass gave way before him; but before he got quite through, Gregson, Lestrade, and Holmes sprang upon him like so many staghounds. He was dragged back into the room, and then commenced a terrific conflict. So powerful and so fierce was he that the four of us were shaken off again and again. He appeared to have the convulsive strength of a man in an epileptic fit. His face and hands were terribly mangled by his passage through the glass, but loss of blood had no effect in diminishing his resistance. It was not until Lestrade succeeded in getting his hand inside his neckcloth and half-strangling him that we made him realize that his struggles were of no avail; and even then we felt no security until we had pinioned his feet as well as his hands. That done, we rose to our feet breathless and panting.

"We have his cab," said Sherlock Holmes. "It will serve to take him to Scotland Yard. And now, gentlemen," he continued, with a pleasant smile, "we have reached the end of our little mystery. You are very welcome to put any questions that you like to me now, and there is no danger that I will refuse to answer them."

"When I got to London my pocket was about empty, and I found that I must turn my hand to something for my living. Driving and riding are as natural to me as walking, so I applied at a cab-owner's office, and soon got employment. I was to bring a certain sum a week to the owner, and whatever was over that I might keep for myself. There was seldom much over, but I managed to scrape along somehow. The hardest job was to learn my way about, for I reckon that of all the mazes that ever were contrived, this city is the most confusing. I had a map beside me, though, and when once I had spotted the principal hotels and stations, I got on pretty well.

"It was some time before I found out where my two gentlemen were living; but I inquired and inquired until at last I dropped across them. They were at a boarding-house at Camberwell, over on the other side of the river. When once I found them out, I knew that I had them at my mercy. I had grown my beard, and there was no chance of their recognizing me. I would dog them and follow them until I saw my opportunity. I was determined that they should not escape me again."

Left *The archway leading to Scotland Yard from Whitehall, c. 1880. The Metropolitan Police had their headquarters here, 1829–90. These premises soon became too cramped, prompting* The Times *to comment, 'Innumerable books are piled up on staircases . . . piles of clothing, saddles and horse furniture, blankets and all manner of things are heaped up in little garrets in a state of what outside Scotland Yard would be called hopeless confusion.'* (Map 3, N 20)

Above *The entrance to a boarding-house for single men in the Camberwell Road. These photographs of the boarding-house and one of its bedrooms (right) were taken in 1901. Camberwell was a rural village during the eighteenth century, but by the late nineteenth century had been absorbed into the urban sprawl of South London.* (Map 2, Q–R 22)

"Presently some luggage was brought out and after a time Drebber and Stangerson followed it, and drove off. I whipped up my horse and kept within sight of them, feeling very ill at ease, for I feared that they were going to shift their quarters. At Euston Station they got out, and I left a boy to hold my horse and followed them on to the platform. I heard them ask for the Liverpool train, and the guard answer that one had just gone, and there would not be another for some hours."

Opened in 1837, Euston Station was the first of London's major rail termini. At the entrance to the station lay the famous Euston Arch, which was demolished in 1963 against massive public opposition. The photographs of the Arch (right) and platforms (below) were taken in the 1890s. (Map 3, J–K 19)

Top right *Waterloo Bridge in 1896. Constructed between 1811 and 1817, to the designs of John Rennie, it was described as 'the noblest bridge on earth'. The imposing building seen to the right of the bridge is Somerset House. Waterloo Bridge was demolished in 1936 and replaced by the current structure. (Map 3, M 20)*

Bottom right *'Growlers' outside a suburban London station in 1895. The growler, a four-wheeled cab drawn by a single horse, seated two people inside the cab and, if necessary, a third beside the driver.*

"He walked down the road and went into one or two liquor shops, staying for nearly half an hour in the last of them. When he came out, he staggered in his walk, and was evidently pretty well on. There was a hansom just in front of me, and he hailed it. I followed it so close that the nose of my horse was within a yard of his driver the whole way. We rattled across Waterloo Bridge and through miles of streets, until, to my astonishment, we found ourselves back in the terrace in which he had boarded. I could not imagine what his intention was in returning there; but I went on and pulled up my cab a hundred yards or so from the house. He entered it, and his hansom drove away."

The Conclusion

. . . "Now let me endeavour to show you the different steps in my reasoning. To begin at the beginning. I approached the house, as you know, on foot, and with my mind entirely free from all impressions. I naturally began by examining the roadway, and there, as I have already explained to you, I saw clearly the marks of a cab, which, I ascertained by inquiry, must have been there during the night. I satisfied myself that it was a cab and not a private carriage by the narrow gauge of the wheels. The ordinary London growler is considerably less wide than a gentleman's brougham."

The Sign of Four

"You have an extraordinary genius for minutiæ," I remarked.

"I appreciate their importance. Here is my monograph upon the tracing of footsteps, with some remarks upon the uses of plaster of Paris as a preserver of impresses. Here, too, is a curious little work upon the influence of a trade upon the form of the hand, with lithotypes of the hands of slaters, sailors, cork-cutters, compositors, weavers, and diamond-polishers. That is a matter of great practical interest to the scientific detective—especially in cases of unclaimed bodies, or in discovering the antecedents of criminals. But I weary you with my hobby."

"Not at all," I answered earnestly. "It is of the greatest interest to me, especially since I have had the opportunity of observing your practical application of it. But you spoke just now of observation and deduction. Surely the one to some extent implies the other."

"Why, hardly," he answered, leaning back luxuriously in his armchair and sending up thick blue wreaths from his pipe. "For example, observation shows me that you have been to the Wigmore Street Post-Office this morning, but deduction lets me know that when there you dispatched a telegram."

Below *Wigmore Street in 1910. (Map 3, L 17–18)*

Left *The Langham Hotel,
Langham Place, in 1885.
Completed in 1864, and
extravagantly furnished in gold,
scarlet and white, it rapidly
established itself as a leading
society hotel. Mark Twain,
Arnold Bennett, Frank Harris
and Napoleon III of France
were among the many famous
guests who stayed here.
(Map 3, L 18)*

Far right *The Strand, c. 1900.
This famous street, which runs
between Charing Cross and the
Law Courts, was described by
Disraeli as 'the finest street in
Europe'. In the late nineteenth
century it was renowned for its
many theatres and restaurants.
(Map 3, M 20)*

Below right *Wellington Street
in 1902. The pillared building
in the centre of the photograph is
the Lyceum Theatre.
(Map 3, M 20)*

"Briefly," she continued, "the facts are these. My father was an officer in an Indian regiment, who sent me home when I was quite a child. My mother was dead, and I had no relative in England. I was placed, however, in a comfortable boarding establishment at Edinburgh, and there I remained until I was seventeen years of age. In the year 1878 my father, who was senior captain of his regiment, obtained twelve months' leave and came home. He telegraphed to me from London that he had arrived all safe and directed me to come down at once, giving the Langham Hotel as his address. His message, as I remember, was full of kindness and love. On reaching London I drove to the Langham and was informed that Captain Morstan was staying there, but

that he had gone out the night before and had not returned. I waited all day without news of him. That night, on the advice of the manager of the hotel, I communicated with the police, and next morning we advertised in all the papers. Our inquiries led to no result; and from that day to this no word has ever been heard of my unfortunate father. He came home with his heart full of hope to find some peace, some comfort, and instead—"

She put her hand to her throat, and a choking sob cut short the sentence.

"The date?" asked Holmes, opening his notebook.

"He disappeared upon the third of December, 1878—nearly ten years ago."

It was a September evening and not yet seven o'clock, but the day had been a dreary one, and a dense drizzly fog lay low upon the great city. Mud-coloured clouds drooped sadly over the muddy streets. Down the Strand the lamps were but misty splotches of diffused light which threw a feeble circular glimmer upon the slimy pavement. The yellow glare from the shop-windows streamed out into the steamy, vaporous air and threw a murky, shifting radiance across the crowded thoroughfare. There was, to my mind, something eerie and ghostlike in the endless procession of faces which flitted across these narrow bars of light—sad faces and glad, haggard and merry. Like all humankind, they flitted from the gloom into the light and so back into the gloom once more. I am not subject to impressions, but the dull, heavy evening, with the strange business upon which we were engaged, combined to make me nervous and depressed.

At the Lyceum Theatre the crowds were already thick at the side-entrances. In front a continuous stream of hansoms and four-wheelers were rattling up, discharging their cargoes of shirt-fronted men and beshawled, bediamonded women. We had hardly reached the third pillar, which was our rendezvous, before a small, dark, brisk man in the dress of a coachman accosted us.

At first I had some idea as to the direction in which we were driving; but soon, what with our pace, the fog, and my own limited knowledge of London, I lost my bearings and knew nothing save that we seemed to be going a very long way. Sherlock Holmes was never at fault, however, and he muttered the names as the cab rattled through squares and in and out by tortuous by-streets.

"Rochester Row," said he. "Now Vincent Square. Now we come out on the Vauxhall Bridge Road. We are making for the Surrey side apparently. Yes, I thought so. Now we are on the bridge. You can catch glimpses of the river."

We did indeed get a fleeting view of a stretch of the Thames, with the lamps shining upon the broad, silent water; but our cab dashed on and was soon involved in a labyrinth of streets upon the other side.

"Wandsworth Road," said my companion. "Priory Road. Lark Hall Lane. Stockwell Place. Robert Street. Cold Harbour Lane. Our quest does not appear to take us to very fashionable regions."

Left Almshouses in Rochester Row, *1891. Named after the Bishops of Rochester, the almshouses were constructed in 1881. (Map 3, O 19)*

Above A scene in Coldharbour Lane, *c. 1900. The sign in the window of the fish restaurant (right) reveals that the national taste for fried fish is by no means a contemporary phenomenon. (Map 2, S 22)*

We had indeed reached a questionable and forbidding neighbourhood. Long lines of dull brick houses were only relieved by the coarse glare and tawdry brilliancy of public-houses at the corner.

Below *The Three Goats' Heads pub in Wandsworth Road, c. 1890. This ornate building is a fine example of a late Victorian public house. (Map 2, S 18)*

. . . "I have seen something of the rough side of life, but I give you my word that this quick succession of strange surprises to-night has shaken my nerve completely. I should like, however, to see the matter through with you, now that I have got so far."

"Your presence will be of great service to me," he answered. "We shall work the case out independently and leave this fellow Jones to exult over any mare's-nest which he may choose to construct. When you have dropped Miss Morstan, I wish you to go on to No. 3 Pinchin Lane, down near the water's edge at Lambeth. The third house on the right-hand side is a bird-stuffer's; Sherman is the name. You will see a weasel holding a young rabbit in the window. Knock old Sherman up and tell him, with my compliments, that I want Toby at once. You will bring Toby back in the cab with you."

"A dog, I suppose."

"Yes, a queer mongrel with a most amazing power of scent. I would rather have Toby's help than that of the whole detective force of London."

. . . "I had thought of that. But you notice that he keeps on the pavement, whereas the barrel passed down the roadway. No, we are on the true scent now."

It tended down towards the riverside, running through Belmont Place and Prince's Street. At the end of Broad Street it ran right down to the water's edge, where there was a small wooden wharf. Toby led us to the very edge of this and there stood whining, looking out on the dark current beyond.

"We are out of luck," said Holmes. "They have taken to a boat here."

Several small punts and skiffs were lying about in the water and on the edge of the wharf. We took Toby round to each in turn, but though he sniffed earnestly he made no sign.

Close to the rude landing-stage was a small brick house, with a wooden placard slung out through the second window. "Mordecai Smith" was printed across it in large letters, and underneath, "Boats to hire by the hour or day."

Two views of Broad Street showing (right) the upper section in 1908, and (above), in an earlier photograph, dated 1865, the wharf and River Thames beyond. (Map 2, P 20)

Left A waterfront scene at Lambeth prior to the construction of the Embankment. (Map 2, P 20)

"What are we to do, then?" I asked as we landed near Millbank Penitentiary

"Take this hansom, drive home, have some breakfast, and get an hour's sleep. It is quite on the cards that we may be afoot to-night again. Stop at a telegraph office, cabby! We will keep Toby, for he may be of use to us yet."

We pulled up at the Great Peter Street Post-Office, and Holmes dispatched his wire.

Above *Millbank in 1903. Just to the left of this photograph lay the notorious Millbank Penitentiary which was demolished in 1903. (Map 3, O 20)*

Left *Great Peter Street at the junction with Tufton Street. The photograph was taken in 1909. (Map 3, O 19)*

Right *Richmond Bridge in 1900. Completed in 1777 it is the oldest surviving bridge over the Thames in the Greater London area. (Map 1, T 4)*

. . . "I have set other agencies at work and used every means at my disposal. The whole river has been searched on either side, but there is no news, nor has Mrs. Smith heard of her husband. I shall come to the conclusion soon that they have scuttled the craft. But there are objections to that."

"Or that Mrs. Smith has put us on a wrong scent."

"No, I think that may be dismissed. I had inquiries made, and there is a launch of that description."

"Could it have gone up the river?"

"I have considered that possibility, too, and there is a search-party who will work up as far as Richmond. If no news comes to-day I shall start off myself to-morrow and go for the men rather than the boat. But surely, surely, we shall hear something."

We did not, however. Not a word came to us either from Wiggins or from the other agencies.

"Your friend, Mr. Sherlock Holmes, is a wonderful man, sir," said he in a husky and confidential voice. "He's a man who is not to be beat. I have known that young man go into a good many cases, but I never saw the case yet that he could not throw a light upon. He is irregular in his methods and a little quick perhaps in jumping at theories, but, on the whole, I think he would have made a most promising officer, and I don't care who knows it. I have had a wire from him this morning, by which I understand that he has got some clue to this Sholto business. Here is his message."

He took the telegram out of his pocket and handed it to me. It was dated from Poplar at twelve o'clock.

GO TO BAKER STREET AT ONCE [it said]. IF I HAVE NOT RETURNED, WAIT FOR ME. I AM CLOSE ON THE TRACK OF THE SHOLTO GANG. YOU CAN COME WITH US TO-NIGHT IF YOU WANT TO BE IN AT THE FINISH.

Left *Poplar in 1902, showing the imposing entrance to the East India Docks. (Map 4, M 30)*

Below *'Westminster Stairs' – or landing place – lies in the foreground of this photograph of the Embankment, taken in 1890. (Map 3, N 20)*

"How has your case prospered?"

"It has all come to nothing. I have had to release two of my prisoners, and there is no evidence against the other two."

"Never mind. We shall give you two others in the place of them. But you must put yourself under my orders. You are welcome to all the official credit, but you must act on the lines that I point out. Is that agreed?"

"Entirely, if you will help me to the men."

"Well, then, in the first place I shall want a fast police-boat—a steam launch—to be at the Westminster Stairs at seven o'clock."

While this conversation had been proceeding, we had been shooting the long series of bridges which span the Thames. As we passed the City the last rays of the sun were gilding the cross upon the summit of St. Paul's. It was twilight before we reached the Tower.

"That is Jacobson's Yard," said Holmes, pointing to a bristle of masts and rigging on the Surrey side. "Cruise gently up and down here under cover of this string of lighters." He took a pair of night-glasses from his pocket and gazed some time at the shore. "I see my sentry at his post," he remarked, "but no sign of a handkerchief."

Below A view of the Thames taken from London Bridge in the 1880s. The Tower of London can be seen in the distance. Begun by William the Conqueror after 1066 and added to by subsequent monarchs, the Tower has served as prison, palace and place of execution. It now houses the Crown Jewels.

Right The Tower of London, seen from 'Jacobson's Yard' in 1896. (Map 3, M 24)

Bottom right The Thames at Greenwich, c. 1890. Christopher Wren's magnificent Royal Hospital can be seen in the right of the photograph. (Map 6, Q 30)

The dull blur in front of us resolved itself now clearly into the dainty *Aurora*. Jones turned our searchlight upon her, so that we could plainly see the figures upon her deck. One man sat by the stern, with something black between his knees, over which he stooped. Beside him lay a dark mass, which looked like a Newfoundland dog. The boy held the tiller, while against the red glare of the furnace I could see old Smith, stripped to the waist, and shovelling coals for dear life. They may have had some doubt at first as to whether we were really pursuing them, but now as we followed every winding and turning which they took there could no longer be any question about it. At Greenwich we were about three hundred paces behind them. At Blackwall we could not have been more than two hundred and fifty. I have coursed many creatures in many countries during my checkered career, but never did sport give me such a wild thrill as this mad, flying man-hunt down the Thames.

Adventures of
Sherlock Holmes

remarkable, save that the passage window could be reached from the top of the coach-house. I walked round it and examined it closely from every point of view, but without noting anything else of interest."

. . . "And what of Irene Adler?" I asked.

"Oh, she has turned all the men's heads down in that part. She is the daintiest thing under a bonnet on this planet. So say the Serpentine-mews, to a man. She lives quietly, sings at concerts, drives out at five every day, and returns at seven sharp for dinner. Seldom goes out at other times, except when she sings. Has only one male visitor, but a good deal of him. He is dark, handsome, and dashing, never calls less than once a day, and often twice. He is a Mr. Godfrey Norton, of the Inner Temple."

Above *A house in St. John's Wood in the 1880s. During the Victorian era the villas of St. John's Wood often housed the mistresses of gentlemen.* (Map 3, J–K 16)

Right *The Inner Temple, c. 1890. The Temple is strongly associated with the legal profession and many barristers have chambers there.* (Map 3, M 21)

Holmes scribbled a receipt upon a sheet of his note-book and handed it to him.

"And Mademoiselle's address?" he asked.

"Is Briony Lodge, Serpentine Avenue, St. John's Wood."

. . . "I soon found Briony Lodge. It is a *bijou* villa, with a garden at the back, built out in front right up to the road, two stories. Chubb lock to the door. Large sitting-room on the right side, well furnished, with long windows almost to the floor, and those preposterous English window fasteners which a child could open. Behind there was nothing

. . . "He was in the house about half an hour, and I could catch glimpses of him in the windows of the sitting-room, pacing up and down, talking excitedly, and waving his arms. Of her I could see nothing. Presently he emerged, looking even more flurried than before. As he stepped up to the cab, he pulled a gold watch from his pocket and looked at it earnestly, 'Drive like the devil,' he shouted, 'first to Gross & Hankey's in Regent Street, and then to the Church of St. Monica in the Edgware Road. Half a guinea if you do it in twenty minutes!'"

. . . I took the paper from him and read as follows:

Left *Regent Street in the 1890s. Designed by John Nash as an integral part of his scheme to connect Regent's Park with Carlton House, it was completed between 1810 and 1820. The beautiful curved quadrant, seen here, contained many fine shops and was the focal point of Nash's plan. (Map 3, L–M 18–19)*

Above *Fleet Street in 1890. 'Pope's Court' is Poppins Court, which lies at the eastern end of Fleet Street, by Ludgate Circus. (Map 3, M 21)*

To THE RED-HEADED LEAGUE:

On account of the bequest of the late Ezekiah Hopkins, of Lebanon, Pennsylvania, U.S.A., there is now another vacancy open which entitles a member of the League to a salary of £4 a week for purely nominal services. All red-headed men who are sound in body and mind, and above the age of twenty-one years, are eligible. Apply in person on Monday, at eleven o'clock, to Duncan Ross, at the offices of the League, 7 Pope's Court, Fleet Street.

"'Oh,' said he, 'his name was William Morris. He was a solicitor and was using my room as a temporary convenience until his new premises were ready. He moved out yesterday.'

"'Where could I find him?'

"'Oh, at his new offices. He did tell me the address. Yes, 17 King Edward Street, near St. Paul's.'"

"I started off, Mr. Holmes, but when I got to that address it was a manufactory of artificial knee-caps, and no one in it had ever heard of either Mr. William Morris or Mr. Duncan Ross."

Right King Edward Street in 1907. (Map 3, L 22)

. . . "Sarasate plays at the St. James's Hall this afternoon," he remarked. "What do you think, Watson? Could your patients spare you for a few hours?"

"I have nothing to do to-day. My practice is never very absorbing."

"Then put on your hat and come. I am going through the City first, and we can have some lunch on the way. I observe that there is a good deal of German music on the programme, which is rather more to my taste than Italian or French. It is introspective, and I want to introspect. Come along!"

Left The building to the left of the 'Aerated Bread Company' is St. James's Hall, Piccadilly. Completed in 1857, it established itself as London's leading concert hall. It was demolished in 1905. A playbill (near left) advertises the Spanish violinist Pablo Sarasate's concerts for autumn 1896. (Map 3, M 19)

Right Kensington High Street in 1905. (Map 3, N 14)

As I drove home to my house in Kensington I thought over it all, from the extraordinary story of the red-headed copier of the Encyclopædia down to the visit to Saxe-Coburg Square, and the ominous words with which he had parted from me. What was this nocturnal expedition, and why should I go armed? Where were we going, and what were we to do? I had the hint from Holmes that this smooth-faced pawn-broker's assistant was a formidable man—a man who might play a deep game. I tried to puzzle it out, but gave it up in despair until night should bring an explanation.

Left *Oxford Street in the 1890s. In the late nineteenth century Oxford Street developed into the long shopping street familiar to Londoners today, stretching unbroken from Park Lane to St. Giles Circus.* (Map 3, M–L 18–19)

Below *Baker Street in 1896, looking north.* (Map 3, L 17)

It was a quarter-past nine when I started from home and made my way across the Park, and so through Oxford Street to Baker Street. Two hansoms were standing at the door, and as I entered the passage I heard the sound of voices from above. On entering his room I found Holmes in animated conversation with two men, one of whom I recognized as Peter Jones, the official police agent, while the other was a long, thin, sad-faced man, with a very shiny hat and oppressively respectable frock-coat.

"Ha! our party is complete," said Holmes, buttoning up his pea-jacket and taking his heavy hunting crop from the rack. "Watson, I think you know Mr. Jones, of Scotland Yard? Let me introduce you to Mr. Merryweather, who is to be our companion in to-night's adventure."

. . . Sherlock Holmes was not very communicative during the long drive and lay back in the cab humming the tunes which he had heard in the afternoon. We rattled through an endless labyrinth of gas-lit streets until we emerged into Farringdon Street.

"We are close there now," my friend remarked. "This fellow Merryweather is a bank director, and personally interested in the matter. I thought it as well to have Jones with us also. He is not a bad fellow, though an absolute imbecile in his profession."

Below *Farringdon Street in 1898, showing Holborn Viaduct. The viaduct was completed in 1896 at enormous cost and was officially opened by Queen Victoria. On the same day she opened Blackfriars Bridge, which lies at the southern end of Farringdon Street.*
(Map 3, L 21)

"I advertised for him in last Saturday's *Chronicle*," said she. "Here is the slip and here are four letters from him."

"Thank you. And your address?"

"No. 31 Lyon Place, Camberwell."

"Mr. Angel's address you never had, I understand. Where is your father's place of business?"

"He travels for Westhouse & Marbank, the great claret importers of Fenchurch Street."

Left *The Midland Grand Hotel – known as the St. Pancras Hotel – in 1896. Situated in the Euston Road near St. Saviour's Chapel, this magnificent building was completed in 1872 by George Gilbert Scott. (Map 3, J 20)*
Below *Fenchurch Street in 1902. (Map 3, M 23–24)*

. . . "Your wedding was arranged, then, for the Friday. Was it to be in church?"

"Yes, sir, but very quietly. It was to be at St. Saviour's, near King's Cross, and we were to have breakfast afterwards at the St. Pancras Hotel. Hosmer came for us in a hansom, but as there were two of us he put us both into it and stepped himself into a four-wheeler, which happened to be the only other cab in the street. We got to the church first, and when the four-wheeler drove up we waited for him to step out, but he never did, and when the cabman got down from the box and looked there was no one there! The cabman said that he could not imagine what had become of him, for he had seen him get in with his own eyes.

Right *Paddington Station in 1895. It was completed in 1854 to the designs of Isambard Kingdom Brunel, the foremost engineer and architect of the age. (Map 3, L 15)*

We were seated at breakfast one morning, my wife and I, when the maid brought in a telegram. It was from Sherlock Holmes and ran in this way:

HAVE YOU A COUPLE OF DAYS TO SPARE? HAVE JUST BEEN WIRED FOR FROM THE WEST OF ENGLAND IN CONNECTION WITH BOSCOMBE VALLEY TRAGEDY. SHALL BE GLAD IF YOU WILL COME WITH ME. AIR AND SCENERY PERFECT. LEAVE PADDINGTON BY THE 11:15.

"What do you say, dear?" said my wife, looking across at me. "Will you go?"

"I really don't know what to say. I have a fairly long list at present."

"Oh, Anstruther would do your work for you. You have been looking a little pale lately. I think that the change would do you good, and you are always so interested in Mr. Sherlock Holmes's cases."

"I should be ungrateful if I were not, seeing what I gained through one of them," I answered. "But if I am to go, I must pack at once, for I have only half an hour."

My experience of camp life in Afghanistan had at least had the effect of making me a prompt and ready traveller. My wants were few and simple, so that in less than the time stated I was in a cab with my valise, rattling away to Paddington Station. Sherlock Holmes was pacing up and down the platform, his tall, gaunt figure made even gaunter and taller by his long gray travelling-cloak and close-fitting cloth cap.

My eye caught the name of Openshaw, and the heading 'Tragedy Near Waterloo Bridge.' Here is the account:

"Between nine and ten last night Police-Constable Cook, of the H Division, on duty near Waterloo Bridge, heard a cry for help and a splash in the water. The night, however, was extremely dark and stormy, so that, in spite of the help of several passers-by, it was quite impossible to effect a rescue. The alarm, however, was given, and, by the aid of the water-police, the body was eventually recovered. It proved to be that of a young gentleman whose name, as it appears from an envelope which was found in his pocket, was John Openshaw . . ."

We sat in silence for some minutes, Holmes more depressed and shaken than I had ever seen him.

"That hurts my pride, Watson," he said at last. "It is a petty feeling, no doubt, but it hurts my pride. It becomes a personal matter with me now, and, if God sends me health, I shall set my hand upon this gang. That he should come to me for help, and that I should send him away to his death—!" He sprang from his chair and paced about the room in uncontrollable agitation, with a flush upon his sallow cheeks and a nervous clasping and unclasping of his long thin hands.

"They must be cunning devils," he exclaimed at last. "How could they have decoyed him down there? The Embankment is not on the direct line to the station."

. . . "I have spent the whole day," said he, "over Lloyd's registers and files of the old papers, following the future career of every vessel which touched at Pondicherry in January and February in '83. There were thirty-six ships of fair tonnage which were reported there during those months. Of these, one, the *Lone Star*, instantly attracted my attention, since, although it was reported as having cleared from London, the name is that which is given to one of the states of the Union."

"The *Lone Star* had arrived here last week. I went down to the Albert Dock and found that she had been taken down the river by the early tide this morning, homeward bound to Savannah. I wired to Gravesend and learned that she had passed some time ago, and as the wind is easterly I have no doubt that she is now past the Goodwins and not very far from the Isle of Wight."

Above *The underwriters' room at Lloyds, Royal Exchange in 1909. Lloyds specialised, and still specialises, in marine insurance. (Map 3, M 23)*

Right *Shipping off Gravesend in 1880.*

Left *The Embankment by night, photographed on a very long exposure by Paul Martin, a prizewinning Victorian photographer. The embanking of the Thames for 3½ miles – in the process reclaiming some 32 acres of land – was a colossal achievement of Victorian engineering and construction. It was supervised by Sir Joseph Bazalgette and completed in 1874. (Map 3, N–M 20)*

Upper Swandam Lane is a vile alley lurking behind the high wharves which line the north side of the river to the east of London Bridge. Between a slop-shop and a gin-shop, approached by a steep flight of steps leading down to a black gap like the mouth of a cave, I found the den of which I was in search. Ordering my cab to wait, I passed down the steps, worn hollow in the centre by the ceaseless tread of drunken feet; and by the light of a flickering oil-lamp above the door I found the latch and made my way into a long, low room, thick and heavy with the brown opium smoke, and terraced with wooden berths, like the forecastle of an emigrant ship.

Below *Pauls Wharf seen from the Thames, c. 1870.*
(Map 3, M 22)

Right *'Upper Swandam Lane' is Upper Thames Street, the rear of which is seen here, in 1902.*
(Map 3, M 22–23)

. . . "Had I been recognized in that den my life would not have been worth an hour's purchase; for I have used it before now for my own purposes, and the rascally lascar who runs it has sworn to have vengeance upon me. There is a trap-door at the back of that building, near the corner of Paul's Wharf, which could tell some strange tales of what has passed through it upon the moonless nights."

"What! You do not mean bodies?"

"Ay, bodies, Watson. We should be rich men if we had £1000 for every poor devil who has been done to death in that den. It is the vilest murder-trap on the whole riverside, and I fear that Neville St. Clair has entered it never to leave it more."

. . . "Some years ago—to be definite, in May, 1884—there came to Lee a gentleman, Neville St. Clair by name, who appeared to have plenty of money. He took a large villa, laid out the grounds very nicely, and lived generally in good style. By degrees he made friends in the neighbourhood, and in 1887 he married the daughter of a local brewer, by whom he now has two children. He had no occupation, but was interested in several companies and went into town as a rule in the morning, returning by the 5:14 from Cannon Street every night."

Right *Commuters outside Cannon Street Station, c. 1895. Completed in 1866, it was designed as the City of London terminus for the South Eastern Railway. (Map 3, M 23)*

Below *Upper Thames Street ('Upper Swandam Lane') in 1910. (Map 3, M 22–23)*

"Last Monday Mr. Neville St. Clair went into town rather earlier than usual, remarking before he started that he had two important commissions to perform, and that he would bring his little boy home a box of bricks. Now, by the merest chance, his wife received a telegram upon this same Monday, very shortly after his departure, to the effect that a small parcel of considerable value which she had been expecting was waiting for her at the offices of the Aberdeen Shipping Company. Now, if you are well up in your London, you will know that the office of the company is in Fresno Street, which branches out of Upper Swandam Lane, where you found me to-night. Mrs. St. Clair had her lunch, started for the City, did some shopping, proceeded to the company's office, got her packet, and found herself at exactly 4:35 walking through Swandam Lane on her way back to the station. Have you followed me so far?"

. . . "Now for the sinister cripple who lives upon the second floor of the opium den, and who was certainly the last human being whose eyes rested upon Neville St. Clair. His name is Hugh Boone, and his hideous face is one which is familiar to every man who goes much to the City. He is a professional beggar, though in order to avoid the police regulations he pretends to a small trade in wax vestas. Some little distance down Threadneedle Street, upon the left-hand side, there is, as you may have remarked, a small angle in the wall. Here it is that this creature takes his daily seat, cross-legged, with his tiny stock of matches on his lap, and as he is a piteous spectacle a small rain of charity descends into the greasy leather cap which lies upon the pavement beside him. I have watched the fellow more than once before ever I thought of making his professional acquaintance, and I have been surprised at the harvest which he has reaped in a short time."

Below *Threadneedle Street in 1898. (Map 3, M 23)*

. . . He snatched it from her in his eagerness, and smoothing it out upon the table he drew over the lamp and examined it intently. I had left my chair and was gazing at it over his shoulder. The envelope was a very coarse one and was stamped with the Gravesend postmark and with the date of that very day, or rather of the day before, for it was considerably after midnight.

"Coarse writing," murmured Holmes. "Surely this is not your husband's writing, madam."

In town the earliest risers were just beginning to look sleepily from their windows as we drove through the streets of the Surrey side. Passing down the Waterloo Bridge Road we crossed over the river, and dashing up Wellington Street wheeled sharply to the right and found ourselves in Bow Street. Sherlock Holmes was well known to the force, and the two constables at the door saluted him. One of them held the horse's head while the other led us in.

. . . It was a bitter night, so we drew on our ulsters and wrapped cravats about our throats. Outside, the stars were shining coldly in a cloudless sky, and the breath of the passers-by blew out into smoke like so many pistol shots. Our footfalls rang out crisply and loudly as we swung through the doctors' quarter, Wimpole Street, Harley Street, and so through Wigmore Street into Oxford Street. In a quarter of an hour we were in Bloomsbury at the Alpha Inn, which is a small public-house at the corner of one of the streets which runs down into Holborn. Holmes pushed open the door of the private bar and ordered two glasses of beer from the ruddy-faced, white-aproned landlord.

"Your beer should be excellent if it is as good as your geese," said he.

"My geese!" The man seemed surprised.

"Yes. I was speaking only half an hour ago to Mr. Henry Baker, who was a member of your goose club."

"Ah! yes, I see. But you see, sir, them's not *our* geese."

"Indeed! Whose, then?"

"Well, I got the two dozen from a salesman in Covent Garden."

"Indeed? I know some of them. Which was it?"

"Breckinridge is his name."

"Ah! I don't know him. Well, here's your good health, landlord, and prosperity to your house. Good-night."

"Now for Mr. Breckinridge," he continued, buttoning up his coat as we came out into the frosty air. "Remember, Watson, that though we have so homely a thing as a goose at one end of this chain, we have at the other a man who will certainly get seven years' penal servitude unless we can establish his innocence. It is possible that our inquiry may but confirm his guilt; but, in any case, we have a line of investigation which has been missed by the police, and which a singular chance has placed in our hands. Let us follow it out to the bitter end. Faces to the south, then, and quick march!"

Left *The 'Alpha Inn' is almost certainly the Museum Tavern opposite the British Museum. This photograph was taken in* 1890. *(Map 3, L 20)*

Opposite *Oxford Street c. 1910. (Map 3, M–L 18–19)*

Left *Covent Garden market in 1891. The market came into existence in the seventeenth century, and evolved into London's best known fruit and vegetable market – though there are records of traders in poultry. In 1973 the market moved to Nine Elms. Covent Garden is now a major tourist attraction.* (Map 3, M 20)

Above *Endell Street in 1913.* (Map 3, L 20)

We passed across Holborn, down Endell Street, and so through a zigzag of slums to Covent Garden Market. One of the largest stalls bore the name of Breckinridge upon it, and the proprietor, a horsy-looking man, with a sharp face and trim side-whiskers, was helping a boy to put up the shutters.

"Good-evening. It's a cold night," said Holmes.

The salesman nodded and shot a questioning glance at my companion.

Left *Kilburn High Road in 1889. (Map 5, I 13–14)*

Above *Brixton Road in 1888. (Map 2, T–Q 21)*

. . . "I went out, as if on some commission, and I made for my sister's house. She had married a man named Oakshott, and lived in Brixton Road, where she fattened fowls for the market. All the way there every man I met seemed to me to be a policeman or a detective; and, for all that it was a cold night, the sweat was pouring down my face before I came to the Brixton Road."

. . . "I had a friend once called Maudsley, who went to the bad, and has just been serving his time in Pentonville. One day he had met me, and fell into talk about the ways of thieves, and how they could get rid of what they stole. I knew that he would be true to me, for I knew one or two things about him; so I made up my mind to go right on to Kilburn, where he lived, and take him into my confidence. He would show me how to turn the stone into money."

. . . "I will go when I have said my say. Don't you dare to meddle with my affairs. I know that Miss Stoner has been here. I traced her! I am a dangerous man to fall foul of! See here." He stepped swiftly forward, seized the poker, and bent it into a curve with his huge brown hands.

"See that you keep yourself out of my grip," he snarled, and hurling the twisted poker into the fireplace he strode out of the room.

"He seems a very amiable person," said Holmes, laughing. "I am not quite so bulky, but if he had remained I might have shown him that my grip was not much more feeble than his own." As he spoke he picked up the steel poker and, with a sudden effort, straightened it out again.

"Fancy his having the insolence to confound me with the official detective force! This incident gives zest to our investigation, however, and I only trust that our little friend will not suffer from her imprudence in allowing this brute to trace her. And now, Watson, we shall order breakfast, and afterwards I shall walk down to Doctors' Commons, where I hope to get some data which may help us in this matter."

. . . "And now, Watson, this is too serious for dawdling, especially as the old man is aware that we are interesting ourselves in his affairs; so if you are ready, we shall call a cab and drive to Waterloo. I should be very much obliged if you would slip your revolver into your pocket. An Eley's No. 2 is an excellent argument with gentlemen who can twist steel pokers into knots. That and a tooth-brush are, I think, all that we need."

Above Holmes would have inspected the will of Dr. Roylott's deceased wife at the Probate Registry Office in Somerset House, seen here in 1899. (Map 3, M 20)

Left Waterloo Station in 1900. Opened in 1848, the terminus was handling over 700 trains a day by the turn of the century. (Map 3, N 21)

Top right A scene in Greenwich, c. 1900. (Map 6, Q 29–30)

Right Victoria Street. Described in 1890 as being, 'lined with lofty mansions . . . and large blocks of chambers', Victoria Street was completed in the 1880s and contained many offices of small businesses. (Map 3, O 18–19)

. . . Holmes sat in his big armchair with the weary, heavy-lidded expression which veiled his keen and eager nature, while I sat opposite to him, and we listened in silence to the strange story which our visitor detailed to us.

"You must know," said he, "that I am an orphan and a bachelor, residing alone in lodgings in London. By profession I am a hydraulic engineer, and I have had considerable experience of my work during the seven years that I was apprenticed to Venner & Matheson, the well-known firm, of Greenwich. Two years ago, having served my time, and having also come into a fair sum of money through my poor father's death, I determined to start in business for myself and took professional chambers in Victoria Street."

. . . "Anything else?" asked Holmes, yawning.

"Oh, yes; plenty. Then there is another note in the *Morning Post* to say that the marriage would be an absolutely quiet one, that it would be at St. George's, Hanover Square, that only half a dozen intimate friends would be invited, and that the party would return to the furnished house at Lancaster Gate which has been taken by Mr. Aloysius Doran."

. . . "And she was afterwards seen walking into Hyde Park in company with Flora Millar, a woman who is now in custody, and who had already made a disturbance at Mr. Doran's house that morning."

"Ah, yes. I should like a few particulars as to this young lady, and your relations to her."

Lord St. Simon shrugged his shoulders and raised his eyebrows. "We have been on a friendly footing for some years—I may say on a *very* friendly footing."

"Who ever heard of such a mixed affair? Every clue seems to slip through my fingers. I have been at work upon it all day."

"And very wet it seems to have made you," said Holmes, laying his hand upon the arm of the pea-jacket.

"Yes, I have been dragging the Serpentine."

"In heaven's name, what for?"

"In search of the body of Lady St. Simon."

Sherlock Holmes leaned back in his chair and laughed heartily.

"Have you dragged the basin of Trafalgar Square fountain?" he asked.

"Why? What do you mean?"

"Because you have just as good a chance of finding this lady in the one as in the other."

Above *The Serpentine in Hyde Park, seen here in 1897, is an artificial lake. Created in 1730, it became a popular boating venue during the Victorian era.* (Map 3, N 16)

Right *Trafalgar Square in 1902. The Square, which contains two fountains, was laid out in 1840 to commemorate Nelson's famous victory over the French and Spanish fleets in 1805, and has as its centrepiece one of the capital's most famous landmarks, Nelson's Column. The National Gallery can be seen behind the fountain.* (Map 3, M 19)

Above left *St. George's, Hanover Square in 1896. Completed in 1724 to the designs of John James, it was a popular venue for society weddings in the Victorian era.* (Map 3, M 18)

Left *Rotten Row, Hyde Park seen in 1890.* (Map 3, N 16)

. . . "Pray compose yourself, sir," said Holmes, "and let me have a clear account of who you are and what it is that has befallen you."

"My name," answered our visitor, "is probably familiar to your ears. I am Alexander Holder, of the banking firm of Holder & Stevenson, of Threadneedle Street."

The name was indeed well known to us as belonging to the senior partner in the second largest private banking concern in the City of London. What could have happened, then, to bring one of the foremost citizens of London to this most pitiable pass? We waited, all curiosity, until with another effort he braced himself to tell his story.

"I feel that time is of value," said he; "that is why I hastened here when the police inspector suggested that I should secure your co-operation. I came to Baker Street by the Underground and hurried from there on foot, for the cabs go slowly through this snow."

Above *The interior of a bank in Threadneedle Street, 1900. (Map 3, M 23)*

Right *The exterior of Baker Street Underground Station in 1895. (Map 3, K 17)*

. . . "When evening came I felt that it would be an imprudence to leave so precious a thing in the office behind me. Bankers' safes had been forced before now, and why should not mine be? If so, how terrible would be the position in which I should find myself! I determined, therefore, that for the next few days I would always carry the case backward and forward with me, so that it might never be really out of my reach. With this intention, I called a cab and drove out to my house at Streatham, carrying the jewel with me. I did not breathe freely until I had taken it upstairs and locked it in the bureau of my dressing-room."

Above *Streatham in 1897. During the eighteenth and early nineteenth centuries many fine Georgian mansions and Regency villas were built in the small village of Streatham. The advent of the railways brought easy access to central London, and many new estates were built to accommodate the rapidly expanding population.* (Map 7, X 19–20)

Memoirs of Sherlock Holmes

Silver Blaze ∘ The Yellow Face ∘ The Stock-broker's Clerk
The "Gloria Scott" ∘ The Musgrave Ritual ∘ The Resident Patient
The Greek Interpreter ∘ The Naval Treaty ∘ The Final Problem

Silver Blaze

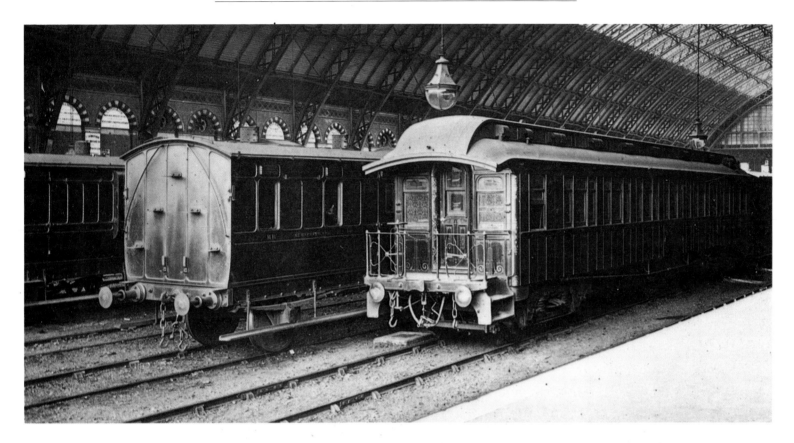

Above *A Pullman car at a London main line station in 1885. These luxurious railway carriages were invented in 1874 by George Pullman of Chicago.*

Right *Clapham Junction in 1890. Opened in 1863, it has developed into the busiest railway intersection in the world. (Map 2, S 16)*

We had the corner of a Pullman car to ourselves that evening as we whirled back to London, and I fancy that the journey was a short one to Colonel Ross as well as to myself as we listened to our companion's narrative of the events which had occurred at the Dartmoor training-stables upon that Monday night, and the means by which he had unravelled them.

. . . "This is Clapham Junction, if I am not mistaken, and we shall be in Victoria in less than ten minutes. If you care to smoke a cigar in our rooms, Colonel, I shall be happy to give you any other details which might interest you."

Sherlock Holmes was a man who seldom took exercise for exercise's sake. Few men were capable of greater muscular effort, and he was undoubtedly one of the finest boxers of his weight that I have ever seen; but he looked upon aimless bodily exertion as a waste of energy, and he seldom bestirred himself save where there was some professional object to be served. Then he was absolutely untiring and indefatigable.

. . . One day in early spring he had so far relaxed as to go for a walk with me in the Park, where the first faint shoots of green were breaking out upon the elms, and the sticky spear-heads of the chestnuts were just beginning to burst into their five-fold leaves. For two hours we rambled about together, in silence for the most part, as befits two men who know each other intimately.

. . . "They had one child, but the yellow fever broke out badly in the place, and both husband and child died of it. I have seen his death certificate. This sickened her of America, and she came back to live with a maiden aunt at Pinner, in Middlesex."

Above *The Broad Walk,
Regent's Park, c. 1900.
(Map 3, J–K 17–18)*

Left *Pinner, a suburb of
London, seen here in 1902.*

. . . "We hardly exchanged a word during breakfast, and immediately afterwards I went out for a walk that I might think the matter out in the fresh morning air."

"I went as far as the Crystal Palace, spent an hour in the grounds, and was back in Norbury by one o'clock. It happened that my way took me past the cottage, and I stopped for an instant to look at the windows and to see if I could catch a glimpse of the strange face which had looked out at me on the day before."

Below *The Crystal Palace, Sydenham, in 1888. This massive glass conservatory was designed by Joseph Paxton for the Great Exhibition of 1851, held in Hyde Park. It was re-erected in Sydenham in the 1850s and destroyed by fire in 1936.* (Map 7, Y 24)

. . . "It is customary at Mawson's for the clerks to leave at midday on Saturday. Sergeant Tuson, of the City police, was somewhat surprised, therefore, to see a gentleman with a carpet-bag come down the steps at twenty minutes past one. His suspicions being aroused, the sergeant followed the man, and with the aid of Constable Pollock succeeded, after a most desperate resistance, in arresting him. It was at once clear that a daring and gigantic robbery had been committed. Nearly a hundred thousand pounds' worth of American railway bonds, with a large amount of scrip in mines and other companies, was discovered in the bag."

. . . "At last I saw a vacancy at Mawson & Williams's, the great stock-broking firm in Lombard Street. I dare say E. C. is not much in your line, but I can tell you that this is about the richest house in London."

Above *Lombard Street in 1902, named after the Italian merchants from Lombardy who settled in the vicinity in the fourteenth century.* (Map 3, M 23)

Right *A City of London police constable c. 1900.*

Far right *The Board Room at the Admiralty.* (Map 3, N 19–20)

"Such, in a few words, my dear boy, is the history of this terrible business in which I was involved. Next day we were picked up by the brig *Hotspur*, bound for Australia, whose captain found no difficulty in believing that we were the survivors of a passenger ship which had foundered. The transport ship *Gloria Scott* was set down by the Admiralty as being lost at sea, and no word has ever leaked out as to her true fate. After an excellent voyage the *Hotspur* landed us at Sydney, where Evans and I changed our names and made our way to the diggings, where, among the crowds who were gathered from all nations, we had no difficulty in losing our former identities."

An anomaly which often struck me in the character of my friend Sherlock Holmes was that, although in his methods of thought he was the neatest and most methodical of mankind, and although also he affected a certain quiet primness of dress, he was none the less in his personal habits one of the most untidy men that ever drove a fellow-lodger to distraction. Not that I am in the least conventional in that respect myself. The rough-and-tumble work in Afghanistan, coming on top of natural Bohemianism of disposition, has made me rather more lax than befits a medical man. But with me there is a limit, and when I find a man who keeps his cigars in the coal-scuttle, his tobacco in the toe end of a Persian slipper, and his unanswered correspondence transfixed by a jack-knife into the very centre of his wooden mantelpiece, then I begin to give myself virtuous airs.

. . . "When I first came up to London I had rooms in Montague Street, just round the corner from the British Museum, and there I waited, filling in my too abundant leisure time by studying all those branches of science which might make me more efficient."

Above The sitting room of 221b Baker Street, from the Abbey House exhibition of 1951. The room can now be viewed at the Sherlock Holmes pub, Northumberland Avenue. (Map 3, N 20)

Right The British Museum in 1895. Designed by Robert Smirke and completed in 1852, it houses an enormous collection of prints, drawings, antiquities and the world famous Reading Room. Montague Street lies adjacent to the east wing of the museum. (Map 3, L 20)

. . . A minute later we were in the street and walking for home. We had crossed Oxford Street and were halfway down Harley Street before I could get a word from my companion.

Left *Houses in Brook Street, 1906. (Map 3, M 17–18)*

Below *A scene in Harley Street in 1910. The locality is famous for its medical specialists. Conan Doyle himself had rooms near here when he attempted to develop a medical practice. (Map 3, L 18)*

. . . "My name is Dr. Percy Trevelyan," said our visitor, "and I live at 403 Brook Street."

"Are you not the author of a monograph upon obscure nervous lesions?" I asked.

His pale cheeks flushed with pleasure at hearing that his work was known to me.

"I so seldom hear of the work that I thought it was quite dead," said he. "My publishers gave me a most discouraging account of its sale. You are yourself, I presume, a medical man?"

. . . "Mycroft lodges in Pall Mall, and he walks round the corner into Whitehall every morning and back every evening. From year's end to year's end he takes no other exercise, and is seen nowhere else, except only in the Diogenes Club, which is just opposite his rooms."

"I cannot recall the name."

"Very likely not. There are many men in London, you know, who, some from shyness, some from misanthropy, have no wish for the company of their fellows. Yet they are not averse to comfortable chairs and the latest periodicals. It is for the convenience of these that the Diogenes Club was started, and it now contains the most unsociable and unclubable men in town. No member is permitted to take the least notice of any other one. Save in the Stranger's Room, no talking is, under any circumstances, allowed, and three offences, if brought to the notice of the committee, render the talker liable to expulsion. My brother was one of the founders, and I have myself found it a very soothing atmosphere."

We had reached Pall Mall as we talked, and were walking down it from the St. James's end. Sherlock Holmes stopped at a door some little distance from the Carlton, and, cautioning me not to speak, he led the way into the hall. Through the glass panelling I caught a glimpse of a large and luxurious room, in which a considerable number of men were sitting about and reading papers, each in his own little nook. Holmes showed me into a small chamber which looked out into Pall Mall, and then, leaving me for a minute, he came back with a companion whom I knew could only be his brother.

Above *Pall Mall in the 1880s, seen from the St. James's end.* (Map 3 M–N 19)

Right *The Carlton Club at its location in Pall Mall, 1895. Traditionally the Carlton has been the club of the Conservative Party, and virtually all Conservative Prime Ministers have been members. Pall Mall is still celebrated for its large number of clubs.* (Map 3, N 19)

Left *Whitehall looking towards Trafalgar Square.* (Map 3, N 20)

. . . The brother scribbled a note upon a leaf of his pocket-book, and, ringing the bell, he handed it to the waiter.

"I have asked Mr. Melas to step across," said he. "He lodges on the floor above me, and I have some slight acquaintance with him, which led him to come to me in his perplexity. Mr. Melas is a Greek by extraction, as I understand, and he is a remarkable linguist. He earns his living partly as interpreter in the law courts and partly by acting as guide to any wealthy Orientals who may visit the Northumberland Avenue hotels."

Opposite *The 'grand salle' of the Grand Hotel, Northumberland Avenue, in 1910.*

Below *Tourists outside the Hotel Metropole, Northumberland Avenue, boarding a carriage for Hampton Court in 1898.* (Map 3, N 20)

. . . Our hope was that, by taking train, we might get to Beckenham as soon as or sooner than the carriage. On reaching Scotland Yard, however, it was more than an hour before we could get Inspector Gregson and comply with the legal formalities which would enable us to enter the house. It was a quarter to ten before we reached London Bridge, and half past before the four of us alighted on the Beckenham platform. A drive of half a mile brought us to The Myrtles—a large, dark house standing back from the road in its own grounds. Here we dismissed our cab and made our way up the drive together

"The windows are all dark," remarked the inspector. "The house seems deserted."

"Our birds are flown and the nest empty," said Holmes.

Left *New Scotland Yard, by Westminster Bridge, became the headquarters of the Metropolitan Police in 1890. Designed by Norman Shaw, the granite facings were quarried by convicts on Dartmoor. (Map 3, N 20)*

Above *The London–Beckenham train at Beckenham Junction. (Map 7, Z 28)*

Left *Hawthorndene House near Beckenham is a strong candidate for 'The Myrtles'. It was demolished in 1962.*

"I was, as Watson may have told you, in the Foreign Office, and through the influence of my uncle, Lord Holdhurst, I rose rapidly to a responsible position. When my uncle became foreign minister in this administration he gave me several missions of trust, and as I always brought them to a successful conclusion, he came at last to have the utmost confidence in my ability and tact.

"Nearly ten weeks ago—to be more accurate, on the twenty-third of May—he called me into his private room, and, after complimenting me on the good work which I had done, he informed me that he had a new commission of trust for me to execute."

Below *The Foreign Office, seen from St. James's Park in 1894. Built in the Italianate style, it was completed in 1873. (Map 3, N 19)*

Right *The Foreign Ministers' room, seen in 1895.*

Opposite *The glorious main staircase of the Foreign Office, 1896.*

. . . "I wrote two more articles, and then, feeling more drowsy than ever, I rose and walked up and down the room to stretch my legs. My coffee had not yet come, and I wondered what the cause of the delay could be. Opening the door, I started down the corridor to find out. There was a straight passage, dimly lighted, which led from the room in which I had been working, and was the only exit from it. It ended in a curving staircase, with the commissionaire's lodge in the passage at the bottom."

. . . "I was ruined, shamefully, hopelessly ruined. I don't know what I did. I fancy I must have made a scene. I have a dim recollection of a group of officials who crowded round me, endeavouring to soothe me. One of them drove down with me to Waterloo, and saw me into the Woking train. I believe that he would have come all the way had it not been that Dr. Ferrier, who lives near me, was going down by that very train. The doctor most kindly took charge of me, and it was well he did so, for I had a fit in the station, and before we reached home I was practically a raving maniac."

. . . "Mr. Joseph Harrison drove us down to the station, and we were soon whirling up in a Portsmouth train. Holmes was sunk in profound thought and hardly opened his mouth until we had passed Clapham Junction.

"It's a very cheery thing to come into London by any of these lines which run high and allow you to look down upon the houses like this."

I thought he was joking, for the view was sordid enough, but he soon explained himself.

"Look at those big, isolated clumps of buildings rising up above the slates, like brick islands in a lead-coloured sea."

"The board-schools."

"Light-houses, my boy! Beacons of the future! Capsules with hundreds of bright little seeds in each, out of which will spring the wiser, better England of the future."

Left *Waterloo Station in 1906. (Map 3, N 21)*

Below *Downing Street in 1901. No. 10, which can be seen at the end of the street to the right, has been the official residence of British Prime Ministers since 1732. (Map 3, N 19–20)*

Right *Mantua Street Board School in 1905. The railway line between Clapham Junction and Victoria is elevated and looks down on the streets of Battersea to the left. The Mantua Street Board School is a strong candidate for the one remarked upon, rising as it does high above the neighbouring roofs. (Map 2, S 15)*

. . . "Where are we going to now?" I asked as we left the office.

"We are now going to interview Lord Holdhurst, the cabinet minister and future premier of England."

We were fortunate in finding that Lord Holdhurst was still in his chambers in Downing Street, and on Holmes sending in his card we were instantly shown up. The statesman received us with that old-fashioned courtesy for which he is remarkable and seated us on the two luxuriant lounges on either side of the fireplace. Standing on the rug between us, with his slight, tall figure, his sharp features, thoughtful face, and curling hair prematurely tinged with gray, he seemed to represent that not too common type, a nobleman who is in truth noble.

"Then these are your instructions, and I beg, my dear Watson, that you will obey them to the letter, for you are now playing a double-handed game with me against the cleverest rogue and the most powerful syndicate of criminals in Europe. Now listen! You will dispatch whatever luggage you intend to take by a trusty messenger unaddressed to Victoria to-night. In the morning you will send for a hansom, desiring your man to take neither the first nor the second which may present itself. Into this hansom you will jump, and you will drive to the Strand end of the Lowther Arcade, handing the address to the cabman upon a slip of paper, with a request that he will not throw it away. Have your fare ready, and the instant that your cab stops, dash through the Arcade, timing yourself to reach the other side at a quarter-past nine."

It was in vain that I asked Holmes to remain for the evening. It was evident to me that he thought he might bring trouble to the roof he was under, and that that was the motive which impelled him to go. With a few hurried words as to our plans for the morrow he rose and came out with me into the garden, clambering over the wall which leads into Mortimer Street, and immediately whistling for a hansom, in which I heard him drive away.

In the morning I obeyed Holmes's injunctions to the letter. A hansom was procured with such precautions as would prevent its being one which was placed ready for us, and I drove immediately after breakfast to the Lowther Arcade, through which I hurried at the top of my speed. A brougham was waiting with a very massive driver wrapped in a dark cloak, who, the instant that I had stepped in, whipped up the horse and rattled off to Victoria Station. On my alighting there he turned the carriage, and dashed away again without so much as a look in my direction.

Above *Mortimer Street, seen from Langham Place in 1898. (Map 3, L 18)*

Right *Trains at Victoria Station in 1886. From 1862 onwards Victoria Station offered an extensive boat train service to the Continent. (Map 3, O 18)*

Left *The Lowther Arcade in 1890. The Arcade was filled with toyshops, and became a mecca for Victorian children. It was demolished in 1904. (Map 3, M 20)*

The Return of Sherlock Holmes

Park Lane is a frequented thoroughfare; there is a cab stand within a hundred yards of the house. No one had heard a shot. And yet there was the dead man, and there the revolver bullet, which had mushroomed out, as soft-nosed bullets will, and so inflicted a wound which must have caused instantaneous death. Such were the circumstances of the Park Lane Mystery, which were further complicated by entire absence of motive, since, as I have said, young Adair was not known to have any enemy, and no attempt had been made to remove the money or valuables in the room.

In the evening I strolled across the Park, and found myself about six o'clock at the Oxford Street end of Park Lane. A group of loafers upon the pavements, all staring up at a particular window, directed me to the house which I had come to see.

Above *Kensington Park Gate.
Residents of Kensington gain
access to the Park via this
entrance, seen here in the 1890s.*
(Map 3, N 15)

Left *Park Lane seen from the
Oxford Street end in the early
1900s. (Map 3 M 17)*

"Well, sir, if it isn't too great a liberty, I am a neighbour of yours, for you'll find my little bookshop at the corner of Church Street, and very happy to see you, I am sure. Maybe you collect yourself, sir. Here's *British Birds*, and *Catullus*, and *The Holy War*—a bargain, every one of them. With five volumes you could just fill that gap on that second shelf. It looks untidy, does it not, sir?"

I moved my head to look at the cabinet behind me. When I turned again, Sherlock Holmes was standing smiling at me across my study table. I rose to my feet, stared at him for some seconds in utter amazement, and then it appears that I must have fainted for the first and last time in my life. Certainly a gray mist swirled before my eyes, and when it cleared I found my collar-ends undone and the tingling after-taste of brandy upon my lips. Holmes was bending over my chair, his flask in his hand.

"My dear Watson," said the well-remembered voice, "I owe you a thousand apologies. I had no idea that you would be so affected."

. . . He turned over the pages lazily, leaning back in his chair and blowing great clouds from his cigar.

"My collection of M's is a fine one," said he. "Moriarty himself is enough to make any letter illustrious, and here is Morgan the poisoner, and Merridew of abominable memory, and Mathews, who knocked out my left canine in the waiting-room at Charing Cross, and, finally, here is our friend of to-night."

He handed over the book, and I read:

'*Moran, Sebastian, Colonel.* Unemployed. Formerly 1st Bangalore Pioneers. Born London, 1840. Son of Sir Augustus Moran, C.B., once British Minister to Persia. Educated Eton and Oxford. Served in Jowaki Campaign, Afghan Campaign, Charasiab (despatches), Sherpur, and Cabul. Author of *Heavy Game of the Western Himalayas* (1881); *Three Months in the Jungle* (1884). Address: Conduit Street. Clubs: The Anglo-Indian, the Tankerville, the Bagatelle Card Club.'

On the margin was written, in Holmes's precise hand:

'The second most dangerous man in London.'

Above *Church Street, Kensington in 1911*, at the junction with Kensington High Street. Church Street was once a rural lane connecting the villages of Notting Hill and Kensington. By the nineteenth century it had developed into a select residential street with several shops.
(*Map 3, N 14*)

Opposite *Conduit Street in 1903*. Laid out in the eighteenth century, few of the original houses in this fashionable street have survived. Conduit Street boasted many famous residents, including the politician Charles James Fox and Dr. Johnson's biographer James Boswell.
(*Map 3, M 18*)

"I live at Torrington Lodge, Blackheath, with my parents, Mr. Holmes, but last night, having to do business very late with Mr. Jonas Oldacre, I stayed at an hotel in Norwood, and came to my business from there. I knew nothing of this affair until I was in the train, when I read what you have just heard. I at once saw the horrible danger of my position, and I hurried to put the case into your hands. I have no doubt that I should have been arrested either at my city office or at my home. A man followed me from London Bridge Station, and I have no doubt—Great heaven! what is that?"

It was a clang of the bell, followed instantly by heavy steps upon the stair. A moment later, our old friend Lestrade appeared in the doorway. Over his shoulder I caught a glimpse of one or two uniformed policemen outside.

"It was so late that I could not get back to Blackheath, so I spent the night at the Anerley Arms, and I knew nothing more until I read of this horrible affair in the morning."

"What do you make of that?" said Holmes.

"Well, what do *you* make of it?"

"That it was written in a train. The good writing represents stations, the bad writing movement, and the very bad writing passing over points. A scientific expert would pronounce at once that this was drawn up on a suburban line, since nowhere save in the immediate vicinity of a great city could there be so quick a succession of points. Granting that his whole journey was occupied in drawing up the will, then the train was an express, only stopping once between Norwood and London Bridge."

"I tried one or two leads, but could get at nothing which would help our hypothesis, and several points which would make against it. I gave it up at last, and off I went to Norwood.

"This place, Deep Dene House, is a big modern villa of staring brick, standing back in its own grounds, with a laurel-clumped lawn in front of it."

Above *Norwood Junction in the early 1900s. (Map 7, B 24)*

Right *A suburban scene in Norwood in 1900. Norwood was celebrated for the healing qualities of the local Beulah Spa discovered in the early eighteenth century. (Map 7, Z 23–25)*

Top left *Hyde Vale, Blackheath in 1897. (Map 6, S 30–31)*

Left *The Anerley Arms, seen here in 1902, is the building immediately to the left of the foremost telegraph pole. The pub still trades under the same name, and is located in Ridsdale Road, opposite Anerley Station. (Map 7, Z 25)*

"I'm not much of a story-teller," said our visitor, nervously clasping and unclasping his great, strong hands. "You'll just ask me anything that I don't make clear. I'll begin at the time of my marriage last year, but I want to say first of all that, though I'm not a rich man, my people have been at Riding Thorpe for a matter of five centuries, and there is no better known family in the County of Norfolk. Last year I came up to London for the Jubilee, and I stopped at a boardinghouse in Russell Square, because Parker, the vicar of our parish, was staying in it. There was an American young lady there—Patrick was the name—Elsie Patrick. In some way we became friends, until before my month was up I was as much in love as man could be. We were quietly married at a registry office, and we returned to Norfolk a wedded couple."

Above *Russell Square in 1897. It was renowned in the Victorian era for its many hotels and boarding houses. (Map 3, K–L 19–20)*

Left *The Diamond Jubilee of 1897, which celebrated the sixtieth anniversary of Queen Victoria's accession to the throne, marked the apogee of the Victorian era. Here the Queen passes crowds during her procession through the City.*

Right *Liverpool Street Station in the early 1900s. Opened in 1874 for the Great Eastern Railway, it has always been the busiest of London's termini, accommodating a huge influx of commuters to the City of London. (Map 3, L 23)*

"You remember Hilton Cubitt, of the dancing men? He was to reach Liverpool Street at one-twenty. He may be here at any moment. I gather from his wire that there have been some new incidents of importance."

We had not long to wait, for our Norfolk squire came straight from the station as fast as a hansom could bring him. He was looking worried and depressed, with tired eyes and a lined forehead.

The young lady, with great clearness and composure, made
the following curious statement:

"My father is dead, Mr. Holmes. He was James Smith,
who conducted the orchestra at the old Imperial Theatre."

Below *The Imperial Theatre,
Tothill Street, in 1901. The
building was destroyed by fire in
1931. (Map 3, O 19)*

. . . "By the way, that last letter of the Duke's—was it found in the boy's room after he was gone?"

"No, he had taken it with him. I think, Mr. Holmes, it is time that we were leaving for Euston."

Below *Hardwick's Great Hall at Euston Station, completed in 1849, served as a concourse and waiting room. (Map 3, J 19)*

"If you do your work well, Mr. Sherlock Holmes, you will have no reason to complain of niggardly treatment."

My friend rubbed his thin hands together with an appearance of avidity which was a surprise to me, who knew his frugal tastes.

"I fancy that I see your Grace's check-book upon the table," said he. "I should be glad if you would make me out a check for six thousand pounds. It would be as well, perhaps, for you to cross it. The Capital and Counties Bank, Oxford Street branch are my agents."

His Grace sat very stern and upright in his chair and looked stonily at my friend.

"Is this a joke, Mr. Holmes? It is hardly a subject for pleasantry."

The Adventure of Black Peter

Several letters were waiting for Holmes at Baker Street. He snatched one of them up, opened it, and burst out into a triumphant chuckle of laughter.

"Excellent, Watson! The alternative develops. Have you telegraph forms? Just write a couple of messages for me: 'Sumner, Shipping Agent, Ratcliff Highway. Send three men on, to arrive ten to-morrow morning.—Basil.' That's my name in those parts. The other is: 'Inspector Stanley Hopkins, 46 Lord Street, Brixton. Come breakfast to-morrow at nine-thirty. Important. Wire if unable to come.—Sherlock Holmes.' There, Watson, this infernal case has haunted me for ten days. I hereby banish it completely from my presence. To-morrow, I trust that we shall hear the last of it forever."

Left *A typical bank interior in the early 1900s. Capital and Counties' Oxford Street branch was located at no. 125, at the junction with Wardour Street. The bank was acquired by Lloyds in 1918.*

Right *The Ratcliff Highway, c. 1900. The Highway was notorious for organised crime in the nineteenth century.* (Map 4, M 25)

"I can see that you have a strong, natural turn for this sort of thing. Very good, do you make the masks. We shall have some cold supper before we start. It is now nine-thirty. At eleven we shall drive as far as Church Row. It is a quarter of an hour's walk from there to Appledore Towers. We shall be at work before midnight. Milverton is a heavy sleeper, and retires punctually at ten-thirty. With any luck we should be back here by two, with the Lady Eva's letters in my pocket."

Holmes and I put on our dress-clothes, so that we might appear to be two theatre-goers homeward bound. In Oxford Street we picked up a hansom and drove to an address in Hampstead. Here we paid off our cab, and with our great coats buttoned up, for it was bitterly cold, and the wind seemed to blow through us, we walked along the edge of the heath.

Left *Church Row, Hampstead, seen in 1897, with the parish church of St. John beyond. The authors H.G. Wells and Wilkie Collins are numbered among the many famous inhabitants of this attractive eighteenth century street. (Map 5, G 15)*

Bottom left *A general view of Hampstead in 1886, from Fitzjohn's Avenue. 'Appledore Towers' has never been absolutely identified, though the large building surrounded by trees seen in the distance is a strong candidate.*

Right *Hampstead Heath in 1897. This 800-acre open space, situated to the north of the city, was saved for public recreation in 1871.*
(Map 5, E–F 14–16)

I could not have believed that an alarm could have spread so swiftly. Looking back, the huge house was one blaze of light. The front door was open, and figures were rushing down the drive. The whole garden was alive with people, and one fellow raised a view-halloa as we emerged from the veranda and followed hard at our heels. Holmes seemed to know the grounds perfectly, and he threaded his way swiftly among a plantation of small trees, I close at his heels, and our foremost pursuer panting behind us. It was a six-foot wall which barred our path, but he sprang to the top and over. As I did the same I felt the hand of the man behind me grab at my ankle, but I kicked myself free and scrambled over a grass-strewn coping. I fell upon my face among some bushes, but Holmes had me on my feet in an instant, and together we dashed away across the huge expanse of Hampstead Heath. We had run two miles, I suppose, before Holmes at last halted and listened intently. All was absolute silence behind us. We had shaken off our pursuers and were safe.

Holmes had not said one word to me about the tragedy which we had witnessed, but I observed all the morning that he was in his most thoughtful mood, and he gave me the impression, from his vacant eyes and his abstracted manner, of a man who is striving to recall something to his memory. We were in the middle of our lunch, when he suddenly sprang to his feet. "By Jove, Watson, I've got it!" he cried. "Take your hat! Come with me!" He hurried at his top speed down Baker Street and along Oxford Street, until we had almost reached Regent Circus. Here, on the left hand, there stands a shop window filled with photographs of the celebrities and beauties of the day. Holmes's eyes fixed themselves upon one of them, and following his gaze I saw the picture of a regal and stately lady in Court dress, with a high diamond tiara upon her noble head. I looked at that delicately curved nose, at the marked eyebrows, at the straight mouth, and the strong little chin beneath it. Then I caught my breath as I read the time-honoured title of the great nobleman and statesman whose wife she had been. My eyes met those of Holmes, and he put his finger to his lips as we turned away from the window.

Below *Oxford Street and Regent Circus in 1898. (Map 3, L 18)*

Left 'Harding Brothers' is the fictitious name for Ponting Brothers, a famous drapery and fancy goods business established in 1873. In this 1905 photograph the premises can be seen on the left-hand side of Kensington High Street, surmounted by a flag. (Map 3, N 14)

Below Campden House Road in 1904. (Map 3, N 14)

. . . "It all seems to centre round that bust of Napoleon which I bought for this very room about four months ago. I picked it up cheap from Harding Brothers, two doors from the High Street Station."

"There was no name on his clothing, and nothing in his pockets save an apple, some string, a shilling map of London, and a photograph. Here it is."

It was evidently taken by a snapshot from a small camera. It represented an alert, sharp-featured simian man, with thick eyebrows and a very peculiar projection of the lower part of the face, like the muzzle of a baboon.

"And what became of the bust?" asked Holmes, after a careful study of this picture.

"We had news of it just before you came. It has been found in the front garden of an empty house in Campden House Road. It was broken into fragments."

A drive of an hour brought us to the picture-dealer's establishment. He was a small, stout man with a red face and a peppery manner.

"Yes, sir. On my very counter, sir," said he. "What we pay rates and taxes for I don't know, when any ruffian can come in and break one's goods. Yes, sir, it was I who sold Dr. Barnicot his two statues. Disgraceful, sir! A Nihilist plot—that's what I make it. No one but an anarchist would go about breaking statues. Red republicans—that's what I call 'em. Who did I get the statues from? I don't see what that has to do with it. Well, if you really want to know, I got them from Gelder & Co., in Church Street, Stepney. They are a well-known house in the trade, and have been this twenty years."

Below *Saffron Hill, Clerkenwell in 1907. An Italian immigrant colony developed in the area during the nineteenth century, and continues to this day. (Map 3, K 21)*

Right *Church Street, Stepney. Renamed Fournier Street, it was known for the Huguenot silkweavers and artisans who settled here in the eighteenth century. (Map 3, L 24)*

. . . "We have an inspector who makes a specialty of Saffron Hill and the Italian Quarter. Well, this dead man had some Catholic emblem round his neck, and that, along with his colour, made me think he was from the South. Inspector Hill knew him the moment he caught sight of him. His name is Pietro Venucci, from Naples, and he is one of the greatest cut-throats in London. He is connected with the Mafia, which, as you know, is a secret political society, enforcing its decrees by murder."

Opposite *An Italian general store in Saffron Hill, 1902.*

. . . "I fancy Chiswick is an address which is more likely to find him. If you will come with me to Chiswick to-night, Lestrade, I'll promise to go to the Italian Quarter with you to-morrow, and no harm will be done by the delay."

A four-wheeler was at the door at eleven, and in it we drove to a spot at the other side of Hammersmith Bridge. Here the cabman was directed to wait. A short walk brought us to a secluded road fringed with pleasant houses, each standing in its own grounds. In the light of a street lamp we read "Laburnum Villa" upon the gate-post of one of them. The occupants had evidently retired to rest, for all was dark save for a fanlight over the hall door, which shed a single blurred circle on to the garden path. The wooden fence which separated the grounds from the road threw a dense black shadow upon the inner side, and here it was that we crouched.

town, with ten miles of man's handiwork on every side of us, to feel the iron grip of Nature, and to be conscious that to the huge elemental forces all London was no more than the molehills that dot the fields. I walked to the window, and looked out on the deserted street. The occasional lamps gleamed on the expanse of muddy road and shining pavement. A single cab was splashing its way from the Oxford Street end.

"Well, Hopkins, here we are at Charing Cross, and I congratulate you on having brought your case to a successful conclusion. You are going to headquarters, no doubt. I think, Watson, you and I will drive together to the Russian Embassy."

Above *A hansom cab in Baker Street, c. 1900. (Map 3, L 17)*

Left *Hammersmith Bridge, photographed by the noted Victorian photographer Henry Taunt in 1895. This decorative and unusual bridge was completed in 1887 to the designs of Joseph Bazalgette. (Map 1, P 11)*

Right *Charing Cross Station in 1899. Completed in 1864 to the designs of John Hawkshaw, it was the London terminus of the South Eastern Railway. In 1906 the arch above the tracks collapsed causing great damage and loss of life. (Map 3, M 20)*

It was a wild, tempestuous night, towards the close of November. Holmes and I sat together in silence all the evening, he engaged with a powerful lens deciphering the remains of the original inscription upon a palimpsest, I deep in a recent treatise upon surgery. Outside the wind howled down Baker Street, while the rain beat fiercely against the windows. It was strange there, in the very depths of the

. . . "Then he went downstairs, said a few words to the man who was waiting in the hall, and the two of them went off together. The last that the porter saw of them, they were almost running down the street in the direction of the Strand."

. . . "Who are you, sir?"

"I am Cyril Overton."

"Then it is you who sent me a telegram. My name is Lord Mount-James. I came round as quickly as the Bayswater bus would bring me. So you have instructed a detective?"

"Yes, sir."

"And are you prepared to meet the cost?"

"I have no doubt, sir, that my friend Godfrey, when we find him, will be prepared to do that."

"But if he is never found, eh? Answer me that!"

. . . "We progress, my dear Watson, we progress. I had seven different schemes for getting a glimpse of that telegram, but I could hardly hope to succeed the very first time."

"And what have you gained?"

"A starting-point for our investigation." He hailed a cab. "King's Cross Station," said he.

"We have a journey, then?"

"Yes, I think we must run down to Cambridge together. All the indications seem to me to point in that direction."

Left *A Bayswater bus, seen in 1890 on a hot summer's day.*

Below *King's Cross Station in 1895. Completed in 1852, to the designs of Lewis Cubbitt, it served as the London terminus for the Great Northern Railway. (Map 3, J 20)*

There was a telegraph-office at a short distance from the hotel. We halted outside it.

"It's worth trying, Watson," said Holmes. "Of course, with a warrant we could demand to see the counterfoils, but we have not reached that stage yet. I don't suppose they remember faces in so busy a place. Let us venture it."

"I am sorry to trouble you," said he, in his blandest manner, to the young woman behind the grating; "there is some small mistake about a telegram I sent yesterday. I have had no answer, and I very much fear that I must have omitted to put my name at the end."

Left *The West Strand Telegraph Office in 1897. One of the four famous 'pepper-pot' cupolas, designed by John Nash, can be seen above the building. (Map 3, M 20)*

. . . Ten minutes later we were both in a cab, and rattling through the silent streets on our way to Charing Cross Station. The first faint winter's dawn was beginning to appear, and we could dimly see the occasional figure of an early workman as he passed us, blurred and indistinct in the opalescent London reek. Holmes nestled in silence into his heavy coat, and I was glad to do the same, for the air was most bitter, and neither of us had broken our fast.

Left *Early morning in Regent Street in the late 1890s. Holmes and Watson would have passed down Regent Street en route to Charing Cross Station from Baker Street.*
(Map 3, M 18–19)

Right *Cockspur Street, c. 1900. Situated at the Trafalgar Square end of Pall Mall, it has long been noted for the numerous shipping and travel companies who are located there.*
(Map 3, M 19)

Below *The principal entrance to New Scotland Yard, now called Norman Shaw Building North and South, seen in 1891.*
(Map 3, N 20)

"I think our next scene of operations must be the shipping office of the Adelaide-Southampton line, which stands at the end of Pall Mall, if I remember right. There is a second line of steamers which connect South Australia with England, but we will draw the larger cover first."

Holmes's card sent in to the manager ensured instant attention, and he was not long in acquiring all the information he needed.

Holmes left the office of the Adelaide-Southampton company. Thence he drove to Scotland Yard, but, instead of entering, he sat in his cab with his brows drawn down, lost in profound thought. Finally he drove round to the Charing Cross telegraph office, sent off a message, and then, at last, we made for Baker Street once more.

The Adventure of the Second Stain

My friend has so often astonished me in the course of our adventures that it was with a sense of exultation that I realized how completely I had astonished him. He stared in amazement, and then snatched the paper from my hands. This was the paragraph which I had been engaged in reading when he rose from his chair.

MURDER IN WESTMINSTER

A crime of mysterious character was committed last night at 16 Godolphin Street, one of the old-fashioned and secluded rows of eighteenth century houses which lie between the river and the Abbey, almost in the shadow of the great Tower of the Houses of Parliament.

Left *Westminster Abbey seen from the Houses of Parliament in 1895. 'Godolphin Street' is a fictitious address, but Great College Street, which lies immediately to the left of the Abbey in this 1895 photograph, fits the description well. (Map 3, O 19–20)*

Right *King Street, Hammersmith in 1903. (Map 1, P 11)*

Below *A scene at Charing Cross in 1900. (Map 3, M 20)*

. . . As to the arrest of John Mitton, the valet, it was a council of despair as an alternative to absolute inaction. But no case could be sustained against him. He had visited friends in Hammersmith that night. The *alibi* was complete.

Mme. Fournaye, who is of Creole origin, is of an extremely excitable nature, and has suffered in the past from attacks of jealousy which have amounted to frenzy. It is conjectured that it was in one of these that she committed the terrible crime which has caused such a sensation in London. Her movements upon the Monday night have not yet been traced, but it is undoubted that a woman answering to her description attracted much attention at Charing Cross Station on Tuesday morning by the wildness of her appearance and the violence of her gestures.

The
Hound of the Baskervilles

From my small medical shelf I took down the Medical Directory and turned up the name. There were several Mortimers, but only one who could be our visitor. I read his record aloud.

'Mortimer, James, M.R.C.S., 1882, Grimpen, Dartmoor, Devon. House surgeon, from 1882 to 1884, at Charing Cross Hospital. Winner of the Jackson prize for Comparative Pathology, with essay entitled 'Is Disease a Reversion?' Corresponding member of the Swedish Pathological Society. Author of 'Some Freaks of Atavism' (*Lancet*, 1882). 'Do We Progress?' (*Journal of Psychology*, March, 1883). Medical Officer for the parishes of Grimpen, Thorsley, and High Barrow.'

Left *Surgeons perform an operation before medical students at Charing Cross Hospital in the 1890s. (Map 3, M 20)*

The Problem

. . . "After you left I sent down to Stamford's for the Ordnance map of this portion of the moor, and my spirit has hovered over it all day. I flatter myself that I could find my way about."

"A large-scale map, I presume?"

"Very large." He unrolled one section and held it over his knee. "Here you have the particular district which concerns us. That is Baskerville Hall in the middle."

He laid an envelope upon the table, and we all bent over it. It was of common quality, grayish in colour. The address, "Sir Henry Baskerville, Northumberland Hotel," was printed in rough characters; the post-mark "Charing Cross," and the date of posting the preceding evening.

Left Stanfords ('Stamfords'), the world's largest map shop, was established in 1852. Their premises are in Long Acre. The photograph dates from the early 1900s. (Map 3, M 20)

Right Northumberland Avenue, with Nelson's Column visible beyond, in 1898. (Map 3, N 20)

Below The Times Building in Printing House Square. Established in 1785 The Times newspaper was printed on these premises until the 1960s. (Map 3, M 22)

"The detection of types is one of the most elementary branches of knowledge to the special expert in crime, though I confess that once when I was very young I confused the *Leeds Mercury* with the *Western Morning News*. But a *Times* leader is entirely distinctive, and these words could have been taken from nothing else."

. . . "You have lost one of your boots, you say?"

"Well, mislaid it, anyhow. I put them both outside my door last night, and there was only one in the morning. I could get no sense out of the chap who cleans them. The worst of it is that I only bought the pair last night in the Strand, and I have never had them on."

"If you have never worn them, why did you put them out to be cleaned?"

"They were tan boots and had never been varnished. That was why I put them out."

. . . "Your hat and boots, Watson, quick! Not a moment to lose!" He rushed into his room in his dressing-gown and was back again in a few seconds in a frock-coat. We hurried together down the stairs and into the street. Dr. Mortimer and Baskerville were still visible about two hundred yards ahead of us in the direction of Oxford Street.

"Shall I run on and stop them?"

"Not for the world, my dear Watson. I am perfectly satisfied with your company if you will tolerate mine. Our friends are wise, for it is certainly a very fine morning for a walk."

He quickened his pace until we had decreased the distance which divided us by about half. Then, still keeping a hundred yards behind, we followed into Oxford Street and so down Regent Street. Once our friends stopped and stared into a shop window, upon which Holmes did the same.

*Left G.H. Harris's bootshop in the Strand, a strong candidate for the shop at which Sir Henry Baskerville purchased his pair of brown boots. The photograph dates from the 1890s.
(Map 3, M 20)*

*Far left A sale on Oxford Street. Busy shoppers crowd in front of the windows.
(Map 3, M–L 18–19)*

Below A hansom cab of the 1880s. Named after Joseph Hansom, this swift two-seater became a popular form of transport and is synonymous with Victorian London.

*Right Bond Street in 1897. Developed between 1700 and 1720, it rapidly established itself as a luxury shopping street and remains so to this day. Many famous picture galleries have their premises in Bond Street.
(Map 3, M 18)*

"There's our man, Watson! Come along! We'll have a good look at him, if we can do no more."

At that instant I was aware of a bushy black beard and a pair of piercing eyes turned upon us through the side window of the cab. Instantly the trapdoor at the top flew up, something was screamed to the driver, and the cab flew madly off down Regent Street. Holmes looked eagerly round for another, but no empty one was in sight. Then he dashed in wild pursuit amid the stream of the traffic, but the start was too great, and already the cab was out of sight.

. . . "And now, Watson, it only remains for us to find out by wire the identity of the cabman, No. 2704, and then we will drop into one of the Bond Street picture galleries and fill in the time until we are due at the hotel."

. . . "He hailed me at half-past nine in Trafalgar Square. He said that he was a detective, and he offered me two guineas if I would do exactly what he wanted all day and ask no questions. I was glad enough to agree. First we drove down to the Northumberland Hotel and waited there until two gentlemen came out and took a cab from the rank. We followed their cab until it pulled up somewhere near here."

"This very door," said Holmes.

"Well, I couldn't be sure of that, but I dare say my fare knew all about it. We pulled up halfway down the street and waited an hour and a half. Then the two gentlemen passed us, walking, and we followed down Baker Street and along—"

"I know," said Holmes.

"Until we got three-quarters down Regent Street. Then my gentleman threw up the trap, and he cried that I should drive right away to Waterloo Station as hard as I could go. I whipped up the mare and we were there under the ten minutes. Then he paid up his two guineas, like a good one, and away he went into the station. Only just as he was leaving he turned round and he said: 'It might interest you to know that you have been driving Mr. Sherlock Holmes.'"

Above Northumberland Avenue from Trafalgar Square. The Grand Hotel, one of the major hotels in the vicinity and possible candidate for the fictitious 'Northumberland Hotel', can be clearly seen in the left of this 1894 photograph.
(Map 3, M 19)

Right Cabs draw up outside Waterloo Station in 1900.
(Map 3, N 21)

. . . "You will report very carefully to me," said Holmes. "When a crisis comes, as it will do, I will direct how you shall act. I suppose that by Saturday all might be ready?"

"Would that suit Dr. Watson?"

"Perfectly."

"Then on Saturday, unless you hear to the contrary, we shall meet at the ten-thirty train from Paddington."

Above *A train waits on platform 8 at Paddington Station in 1898. (Map 3, L 15)*

Our friends had already secured a first-class carriage and were waiting for us upon the platform.

"No, we have no news of any kind," said Dr. Mortimer in answer to my friend's questions. "I can swear to one thing, and that is that we have not been shadowed during the last two days. We have never gone out without keeping a sharp watch, and no one could have escaped our notice."

"You have always kept together, I presume?"

"Except yesterday afternoon. I usually give up one day to pure amusement when I come to town, so I spent it at the Museum of the College of Surgeons."

Left The exterior of the Royal College of Surgeons, Lincoln's Inn Fields, c. 1900. The 'Museum' is the Hunterian Collection of anatomical and physiological specimens collected by the surgeon John Hunter. (Map 3, L 20)

Death on the Moor

. . . "The surprise was not all on one side, I assure you. I had no idea that you had found my occasional retreat, still less that you were inside it, until I was within twenty paces of the door."

"My footprint, I presume?"

"No, Watson; I fear that I could not undertake to recognize your footprint amid all the footprints of the world. If you seriously desire to deceive me you must change your tobacconist; for when I see the stub of a cigarette marked Bradley, Oxford Street, I know that my friend Watson is in the neighbourhood. You will see it there beside the path. You threw it down, no doubt, at that supreme moment when you charged into the empty hut."

Right An Oxford Street tobacconist. 'Bradleys' is a fictitious name, though Salmon and Gluckstein's premises, seen here in 1904, lay close to Baker Street, at no. 257 Oxford Street. (Map 3, M 17)

. . . "Having conceived the idea he proceeded to carry it out with considerable finesse. An ordinary schemer would have been content to work with a savage hound. The use of artificial means to make the creature diabolical was a flash of genius upon his part. The dog he bought in London from Ross and Mangles, the dealers in Fulham Road. It was the strongest and most savage in their possession."

Left *The Craven Family Hotel, Craven Street in 1906. This is the likely model for the fictitious 'Mexborough Private Hotel' which was patronised by the Stapletons. (Map 3, M 20)*

Above *Fulham Road at Queen's Elm Parade, c. 1900. Tradition has it that the Queen's Elm pub was so named after Queen Elizabeth I sheltered here under an elm tree during a violent storm. (Map 2, P 15)*

"They lodged, I find, at the Mexborough Private Hotel, in Craven Street, which was actually one of those called upon by my agent in search of evidence. Here he kept his wife imprisoned in her room while he, disguised in a beard, followed Dr. Mortimer to Baker Street and afterwards to the station and to the Northumberland Hotel."

His Last Bow

He turned his bulldog eyes upon our visitor. "Are you Mr. John Scott Eccles, of Popham House, Lee?"

"I am."

"We have been following you about all the morning."

"You traced him through the telegram, no doubt," said Holmes.

"Exactly, Mr. Holmes. We picked up the scent at Charing Cross Post-Office and came on here."

Below *Charing Cross Post Office. This photograph was probably taken in the 1920s, but the building remained unchanged from Victorian times. (Map 3, M 20)*

A good deal of clothing with the stamp of Marx and Co., High Holborn, had been left behind. Telegraphic inquiries had been already made which showed that Marx knew nothing of his customer save that he was a good payer.

Below High Holborn in 1895. *This ancient thoroughfare, which has many historical and literary associations, contained many shops and hotels in the late Victorian era. (Map 3, L21)*

Right The British Museum's *Reading Room in 1898. Completed in 1857, it was used by scholars and writers such as Karl Marx and George Bernard Shaw. (Map 3, L20)*

Holmes smiled as he turned up an entry in his notebook.

"I spent a morning in the British Museum reading up on that and other points. Here is a quotation from Eckermann's *Voodooism and the Negroid Religions:*

> *The true voodoo-worshipper attempts nothing of importance without certain sacrifices which are intended to propitiate his unclean gods. In extreme cases these rites take the form of human sacrifices followed by cannibalism. The more usual victims are a white cock, which is plucked in pieces alive, or a black goat, whose throat is cut and body burned.*

"So you see our savage friend was very orthodox in his ritual. It is grotesque, Watson," Holmes added, as he slowly fastened his notebook, "but, as I have had occasion to remark, there is but one step from the grotesque to the horrible."

I picked up the paper which he had thrown back to me and read the paragraph indicated. It was headed, "A Gruesome Packet."

"Miss Susan Cushing, living at Cross Street, Croydon, has been made the victim of what must be regarded as a peculiarly revolting practical joke unless some more sinister meaning should prove to be attached to the incident. At two o'clock yesterday afternoon a small packet, wrapped in brown paper, was handed in by the postman. A cardboard box was inside, which was filled with coarse salt. On emptying this, Miss Cushing was horrified to find two human ears, apparently quite freshly severed."

. . . "We know that this woman has led a most quiet and respectable life at Penge and here for the last twenty years. She has hardly been away from her home for a day during that time."

Left *Penge in 1903. With the re-erection of the Crystal Palace in nearby Sydenham and with easy access to the centre of the capital by rail, Penge had become a fashionable middle-class suburb by the late nineteenth century. (Map 7, Z 25–26)*

Above *Surrey Street Market, Croydon, in 1897. A small market town in the eighteenth century, Croydon had developed into a major suburb of London by the 1890s. (See inset Map 7)*

"Lestrade has got him all right," said Holmes, glancing up at me. "Perhaps it would interest you to hear what he says.

"MY DEAR MR. HOLMES:

"In accordance with the scheme which we had formed in order to test our theories" ["the 'we' is rather fine, Watson, is it not?"] "I went down to the Albert Dock yesterday at 6 P. M. and boarded the S. S. May Day, belonging to the Liverpool, Dublin, and London Steam Packet Company."

Above *Stevedores load a ship at berth in the Albert Dock, c. 1895. Opened in 1880, this dock could accommodate large ocean-going vessels.* (Map 4, M–N 34–36)

"I took to my heels, and I ran after the cab. I had a heavy oak stick in my hand, and I tell you I saw red from the first; but as I ran I got cunning, too, and hung back a little to see them without being seen. They pulled up soon at the railway station. There was a good crowd round the booking-office, so I got quite close to them without being seen. They took tickets for New Brighton. So did I, but I got in three carriages behind them."

Right *Passengers board a train at East Croydon Station in 1901. New Brighton, near Liverpool, was a popular seaside resort during the late nineteenth century.*

Below *An exterior view of East Croydon Station in 1900. (See inset Map 7)*

"Mr. Warren is a timekeeper at Morton and Waylight's, in Tottenham Court Road. He has to be out of the house before seven. Well, this morning he had not gone ten paces down the road when two men came up behind him, threw a coat over his head, and bundled him into a cab that was beside the curb. They drove him an hour, and then opened the door and shot him out. He lay in the roadway so shaken in his wits that he never saw what became of the cab. When he picked himself up he found he was on Hampstead Heath; so he took a bus home, and there he lies now on the sofa, while I came straight round to tell you what had happened."

Left *Tottenham Court Road in 1898, looking north from St. Giles Circus. Immediately to the right of this photograph lay the noted Meux's Brewery, where the Dominion Theatre now stands. (Map 3, L 19)*

Below *Hampstead Heath in 1899. By this time the Heath was a favourite recreation area for Cockney Londoners. (Map 5, E–F 14–16)*

Our official detectives may blunder in the matter of intelligence, but never in that of courage. Gregson climbed the stair to arrest this desperate murderer with the same absolutely quiet and businesslike bearing with which he would have ascended the official staircase of Scotland Yard. The Pinkerton man had tried to push past him, but Gregson had firmly elbowed him back. London dangers were the privilege of the London force.

. . . "Well, Watson, you have one more specimen of the tragic and grotesque to add to your collection. By the way, it is not eight o'clock, and a Wagner night at Covent Garden! If we hurry, we might be in time for the second act."

Above *A police officer ascends the 'official' staircase at New Scotland Yard, c. 1910. Senior officers occupied rooms on the ground floor, while other ranks had offices on the floors above, the most junior being at the very top. The only exception was the Commissioner of the Metropolitan Police who occupied an entire turret at the top of the building.*
(Map 3, N 20)

Right *The Royal Opera House, Covent Garden in 1895. London's leading opera house was completed in 1858 to the designs of E.M. Barry. The present building is the third theatre to stand on the Bow Street site.*
(Map 3, M 20)

. . . "Now, Watson, let us have the facts."

"The man's name was Arthur Cadogan West. He was twenty-seven years of age, unmarried, and a clerk at Woolwich Arsenal."

"Government employ. Behold the link with Brother Mycroft!"

"He left Woolwich suddenly on Monday night. Was last seen by his fiancée, Miss Violet Westbury, whom he left abruptly in the fog about 7:30 that evening. There was no quarrel between them and she can give no motive for his action. The next thing heard of him was when his dead body was discovered by a plate-layer named Mason, just outside Aldgate Station on the Underground system in London."

. . . "Come, Watson! And you, Lestrade, could you favour us with your company for an hour or two? We will begin our investigation by a visit to Aldgate Station. Good-bye, Mycroft. I shall let you have a report before evening, but I warn you in advance that you have little to expect."

Above *The main gates of Woolwich Arsenal in 1890. Weapons have been manufactured here since the sixteenth century. (Map 4, O 36)*

Left *Aldgate Station in 1900. The easternmost station of the Metropolitan Railway, Aldgate was opened in 1884, forming the last link in the Circle Line. (Map 3, L 24)*

Right *London Bridge in 1891, looking towards the City. Completed in 1831 by Sir John Rennie to a design by George Rennie, the bridge was dismantled in the 1960s and reconstructed at Lake Havasu City, Arizona. (Map 3, M 23)*

At London Bridge, Holmes wrote a telegram to his brother, which he handed to me before dispatching it. It ran thus:

SEE SOME LIGHT IN THE DARKNESS, BUT IT MAY POSSIBLY FLICKER OUT. MEANWHILE, PLEASE SEND BY MESSENGER, TO AWAIT RETURN AT BAKER STREET, A COMPLETE LIST OF ALL FOREIGN SPIES OR INTERNATIONAL AGENTS KNOWN TO BE IN ENGLAND, WITH FULL ADDRESS. SHERLOCK.

Caulfield Gardens was one of those lines of flat-faced pillared, and porticoed houses which are so prominent a product of the middle Victorian epoch in the West End of London. Next door there appeared to be a children's party, for the merry buzz of young voices and the clatter of the piano resounded through the night. The fog still hung about and screened us with its friendly shade. Holmes had lit his lantern and flashed it upon the massive door.

. . . "This has involved me in extra trouble, however, and I must ask you for a further advance of five hundred pounds. I will not trust it to the post, nor will I take anything but gold or notes. I would come to you abroad, but it would excite remark if I left the country at present. Therefore I shall expect to meet you in the smoking-room of the Charing Cross Hotel at noon on Saturday. Remember that only English notes, or gold, will be taken."

Above Cornwall ('Caulfield') Gardens in 1902. The houses seen here back on to the overground section of the Circle Line described in the story. (Map 3, O 14)

Left The Charing Cross Hotel in the 1880s. Completed in 1864 to the designs of E.M. Barry, its rooms were richly decorated in the high Victorian style. Charing Cross Station lies behind the hotel. In the foreground can be seen a Victorian replica of the Eleanor Cross, a thirteenth century memorial marking one of the resting places of the cortège of Queen Eleanor, wife of Edward I. (Map 3, M 20)

. . . "He's dying, Dr. Watson," said she. "For three days he has been sinking, and I doubt if he will last the day. He would not let me get a doctor. This morning when I saw his bones sticking out of his face and his great bright eyes looking at me I could stand no more of it. 'With your leave or without it, Mr. Holmes, I am going for a doctor this very hour,' said I. 'Let it be Watson, then,' said he. I wouldn't waste an hour in coming to him, sir, or you may not see him alive."

I was horrified for I had heard nothing of his illness. I need not say that I rushed for my coat and my hat. As we drove back I asked for the details.

"There is little I can tell you, sir. He has been working at a case down at Rotherhithe, in an alley near the river, and he has brought this illness back with him. He took to his bed on Wednesday afternoon and has never moved since. For these three days neither food nor drink has passed his lips."

Left *Simpson's-in-the-Strand. This famous restaurant was opened in 1848, and is seen here in the 1890s shortly before demolition and rebuilding in 1900. From Victorian times Simpson's has specialised in traditional English cooking, notably roast beef. (Map 3, M 20)*

Above *A scene in Rotherhithe in 1907, before slum clearances later in the century. (Map 4, N 26–27)*

. . . "Thank you, Watson, you must help me on with my coat. When we have finished at the police-station I think that something nutritious at Simpson's would not be out of place."

But neither the official police nor Holmes's own small but very efficient organization sufficed to clear away the mystery. Amid the crowded millions of London the three persons we sought were as completely obliterated as if they had never lived. Advertisements were tried, and failed. Clues were followed, and led to nothing. Every criminal resort which Shlessinger might frequent was drawn in vain. His old associates were watched, but they kept clear of him. And then suddenly, after a week of helpless suspense there came a flash of light. A silver-and-brilliant pendant of old Spanish design had been pawned at Bovington's, in Westminster Road.

Above *Westminster Road (properly Westminster Bridge Road) in 1904, with Westminster Bridge and Big Ben seen beyond. The buildings to the right were demolished in 1909 to make way for County Hall, headquarters of the London County Council.* (Map 3, N–O 20–21)

Near right *Houses in the Kennington Road.* (Map 3, O 21)

Far right *A London cab and female passenger in 1905.*

On the evening of the third he rushed into our sitting-room, pale, trembling, with every muscle of his powerful frame quivering with excitement.

"We have him! We have him!" he cried.

He was incoherent in his agitation. Holmes soothed him with a few words and thrust him into an armchair.

"Come, now, give us the order of events," said he.

"She came only an hour ago. It was the wife, this time, but the pendant she brought was the fellow of the other. She is a tall, pale woman, with ferret eyes."

"That is the lady," said Holmes.

"She left the office and I followed her. She walked up the Kennington Road, and I kept behind her. Presently she went into a shop. Mr. Holmes, it was an undertaker's."

My companion started. "Well?" he asked in that vibrant voice which told of the fiery soul behind the cold gray face.

"She was talking to the woman behind the counter. I entered as well. 'It is late,' I heard her say, or words to that effect. The woman was excusing herself. 'It should be there before now,' she answered. 'It took longer, being out of the ordinary.' They both stopped and looked at me, so I asked some question and then left the shop."

"You did excellently well. What happened next?"

"The woman came out, but I had hid myself in a doorway. Her suspicions had been aroused, I think, for she looked round her. Then she called a cab and got in."

. . . "Let us try to reconstruct the situation," said he as we drove swiftly past the Houses of Parliament and over Westminster Bridge. "These villains have coaxed this unhappy lady to London, after first alienating her from her faithful maid. If she has written any letters they have been intercepted. Through some confederate they have engaged a furnished house. Once inside it, they have made her a prisoner, and they have become possessed of the valuable jewellery which has been their object from the first."

Below *The Houses of Parliament, in 1897. Completed in 1860 to the designs of Charles Barry and Augustus Pugin, it is a magnificent example of Victorian Gothic architecture. Westminster Bridge lies to the extreme right of this photograph. (Map 3, N 20)*

Right *A funeral procession in South London in 1899.*

. . . "What time was the funeral? Eight, was it not?" he asked eagerly. "Well, it is 7:20 now. Good heavens, Watson, what has become of any brains that God has given me? Quick, man, quick! It's life or death—a hundred chances on death to one on life. I'll never forgive myself, never, if we are too late!"

Five minutes had not passed before we were flying in a hansom down Baker Street. But even so it was twenty-five to eight as we passed Big Ben, and eight struck as we tore down the Brixton Road. But others were late as well as we. Ten minutes after the hour the hearse was still standing at the door of the house, and even as our foaming horse came to a halt the coffin, supported by three men, appeared on the threshold. Holmes darted forward and barred their way.

"Take it back!" he cried, laying his hand on the breast of the foremost. "Take it back this instant!"

. . . "Now you, with this sporting pose of yours—"

"No, no, don't call it a pose. A pose is an artificial thing. This is quite natural. I am a born sportsman. I enjoy it."

"Well, that makes it the more effective. You yacht against them, you hunt with them, you play polo, you match them in every game, your four-in-hand takes the prize at Olympia."

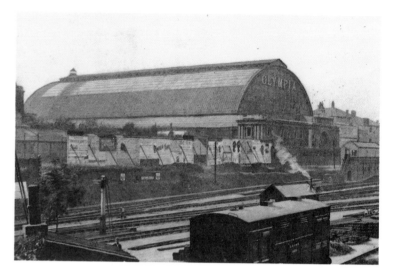

"Must you really go? He may be here any moment."

"No. I'm sorry, but I have already overstayed my time. We shall expect you early to-morrow, and when you get that signal book through the little door on the Duke of York's steps you can put a triumphant finis to your record in England."

Above Olympia *in 1906. This huge amphitheatre, originally called the National Agricultural Hall, opened in 1884. It is an ideal venue for exhibitions, sporting events, and tournaments. The first Horse of the Year Show was held here in 1907.*

Left The Duke of York's Steps, Carlton House Terrace, *c. 1914. The German Embassy was situated at nos. 7–9 Carlton House Terrace, immediately to the left of this photograph. A replica of 'the little door' seen in the centre of this picture, exists along the side of the old German Embassy building opposite. (Map 3, N 19)*

Right An interior view of Claridge's Hotel, Brook Street. *(Map 3, M 18)*

. . . "You can report to me to-morrow in London, Martha, at Claridge's Hotel."

The Case Book of Sherlock Holmes

Both Holmes and I had a weakness for the Turkish bath. It was over a smoke in the pleasant lassitude of the drying-room that I have found him less reticent and more human than anywhere else. On the upper floor of the Northumberland Avenue establishment there is an isolated corner where two couches lie side by side, and it was on these that we lay upon September 3, 1902, the day when my narrative begins. I had asked him whether anything was stirring, and for answer he had shot his long, thin, nervous arm out of the sheets which enveloped him and had drawn an envelope from the inside pocket of the coat which hung beside him.

Below *The 'Northumberland Avenue establishment' referred to was Nevill's Turkish Baths, seen here in an architect's drawing dated 1883.*

Right *Northumberland Avenue at the junction with Craven Street, in 1898. Nevill's lay to the rear of this building in Craven Passage. (Map 3, M 20)*

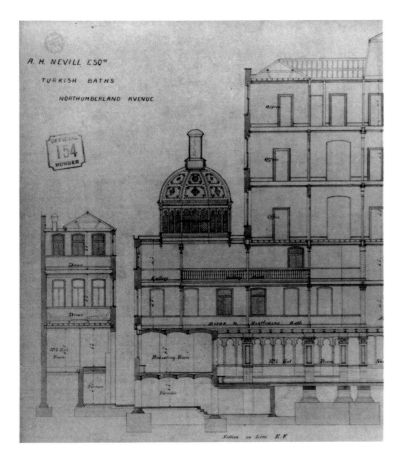

"It may be some fussy, self-important fool; it may be a matter of life or death," said he as he handed me the note. "I know no more than this message tells me."

It was from the Carlton Club and dated the evening before. This is what I read:

"Sir James Damery presents his compliments to Mr. Sherlock Holmes and will call upon him at 4:30 to-morrow. Sir James begs to say that the matter upon which he desires to consult Mr. Holmes is very delicate and also very important. He trusts, therefore, that Mr. Holmes will make every effort to grant this interview, and that he will confirm it over the telephone to the Carlton Club."

"I need not say that I have confirmed it, Watson," said Holmes as I returned the paper. "Do you know anything of this man Damery?"

"Only that this name is a household word in society."

"Well, I can tell you a little more than that. He has rather a reputation for arranging delicate matters which are to be kept out of the papers. You may remember his negotiations with Sir George Lewis over the Hammerford Will case. He is a man of the world with a natural turn for diplomacy. I am bound, therefore, to hope that it is not a false scent and that he has some real need for our assistance."

"Our?"

"Well, if you will be so good, Watson."

"I shall be honoured."

"Then you have the hour—4:30. Until then we can put the matter out of our heads."

I was living in my own rooms in Queen Anne Street at the time, but I was round at Baker Street before the time named. Sharp to the half-hour, Colonel Sir James Damery was announced.

. . . "Apart from what you have told me, can you give me any further information about the man?"

"He has expensive tastes. He is a horse fancier. For a short time he played polo at Hurlingham, but then this Prague affair got noised about and he had to leave. He collects books and pictures. He is a man with a considerable artistic side to his nature. He is, I believe, a recognized authority upon Chinese pottery and has written a book upon the subject."

"A complex mind," said Holmes. "All great criminals have that."

It was not possible for me to follow the immediate steps taken by my friend, for I had some pressing professional business of my own, but I met him by appointment that evening at Simpson's, where, sitting at a small table in the front window and looking down at the rushing stream of life in the Strand, he told me something of what had passed.

Below *Simpson's-in-the-Strand shortly after redecoration in 1900. (Map 3, M 20)*

. . . I think I could show you the very paving-stone upon which I stood when my eyes fell upon the placard, and a pang of horror passed through my very soul. It was between the Grand Hotel and Charing Cross Station, where a one-legged news-vender displayed his evening papers. The date was just two days after the last conversation. There, black upon yellow, was the terrible news-sheet:

MURDEROUS ATTACK UPON
SHERLOCK HOLMES

I think I stood stunned for some moments. Then I have a

Above *Berkeley Square in 1890, looking towards Piccadilly. Laid out in the 1730s, it has always been a highly fashionable London address. (Map 3, M 18)*

Right *The curved building to the right in this 1898 photograph is the Grand Hotel. Charing Cross Station lies beyond on the right. One of London's largest and most spectacular hotels, The Grand boasted a Winter Garden, Palm Court, several restaurants and 500 bedrooms. (Map 3, M 20)*

. . . "There was no difficulty at all about the appointment," said Holmes, "for the girl glories in showing abject filial obedience in all secondary things in an attempt to atone for her flagrant breach of it in her engagement. The General 'phoned that all was ready, and the fiery Miss W. turned up according to schedule, so that at half-past five a cab deposited us outside 104 Berkeley Square, where the old soldier resides—one of those awful gray London castles which would make a church seem frivolous. A footman showed us into a great yellow-curtained drawing-room, and there was the lady awaiting us, demure, pale, self-contained, as inflexible and remote as a snow image on a mountain."

confused recollection of snatching at a paper, of the remonstrance of the man, whom I had not paid, and, finally, of standing in the doorway of a chemist's shop while I turned up the fateful paragraph. This was how it ran:

> We learn with regret that Mr. Sherlock Holmes, the well-known private detective, was the victim this morning of a murderous assault which has left him in a precarious position. There are no exact details to hand, but the event seems to have occurred about twelve o'clock in Regent Street, outside the Café Royal. The attack was made by two men armed with sticks, and Mr. Holmes was beaten about the head and body, receiving injuries which the doctors describe as most serious. He was carried to Charing Cross Hospital and afterwards insisted upon being taken to his rooms in Baker Street. The miscreants who attacked him appear to have been respectably dressed men, who escaped from the bystanders by passing through the Café Royal and out into Glasshouse Street behind it. No doubt they belonged to that criminal fraternity which has so often had occasion to bewail the activity and ingenuity of the injured man.

I need not say that my eyes had hardly glanced over the paragraph before I had sprung into a hansom and was on my way to Baker Street. I found Sir Leslie Oakshott, the famous surgeon, in the hall and his brougham waiting at the curb.

Top right *Glasshouse Street in 1903. The rear entrance to the old Café Royal lay immediately beyond the horse-drawn vehicles shown in the left of this picture. (Map 3, M 19)*

Left *The Café Royal, Regent Street in 1901. This famous restaurant, rebuilt in the 1920s, was synonymous with artistic London of the 1890s. It was patronised by the great writers and artists of the age, including Oscar Wilde, Max Beerbohm, Augustus John and Aubrey Beardsley. (Map 3, M 19)*

Right *An interior view of the London Library, St. James's Square in 1900. The historian Thomas Carlyle founded the* *library in 1841, as an alternative to the library at the British Museum.* *(Map 3, M 19)*

. . . "Now, Watson, I want you to do something for me."

"I am here to be used, Holmes."

"Well, then, spend the next twenty-four hours in an intensive study of Chinese pottery."

He gave no explanations and I asked for none. By long experience I had learned the wisdom of obedience. But when I had left his room I walked down Baker Street, revolving in my head how on earth I was to carry out so strange an order. Finally I drove to the London Library in St. James's Square, put the matter to my friend Lomax, the sublibrarian, and departed to my rooms with a goodly volume under my arm.

I find from my notebook that it was in January, 1903, just after the conclusion of the Boer War, that I had my visit from Mr. James M. Dodd, a big, fresh, sun-burned, upstanding Briton. The good Watson had at that time deserted me for a wife, the only selfish action which I can recall in our association. I was alone.

It is my habit to sit with my back to the window and to place my visitors in the opposite chair, where the light falls full upon them. Mr. James M. Dodd seemed somewhat at a loss how to begin the interview. I did not attempt to help him, for his silence gave me more time for observation. I have found it wise to impress clients with a sense of power, and so I gave him some of my conclusions.

"From South Africa, sir, I perceive."

"Yes, sir," he answered, with some surprise.

"Imperial Yeomanry, I fancy."

"Exactly."

"Middlesex Corps, no doubt."

"That is so. Mr. Holmes, you are a wizard."

I smiled at his bewildered expression.

"When a gentleman of virile appearance enters my room with such tan upon his face as an English sun could never give, and with his handkerchief in his sleeve instead of in his pocket, it is not difficult to place him. You wear a short beard, which shows that you were not a regular. You have the cut of a riding-man. As to Middlesex, your card has already shown me that you are a stockbroker from Throgmorton Street. What other regiment would you join?"

Left *Throgmorton Street in 1905. This busy financial street in the City lies to the north of the Stock Exchange. Thomas Cromwell, Henry VIII's notorious minister, lived here until his execution in 1540. The hall of the Drapers' Company now stands on the site of his house. (Map 3, L 23)*

Right *Madame Tussaud's Waxworks, Marylebone Road, seen in the 1890s. Mme. Tussaud arrived in England from revolutionary France in 1802 and first displayed her lifelike wax figures in Baker Street. The present premises in Marylebone Road were moved to in 1884. The extraordinary likeness of the figures, and the macabre attraction of the Chamber of Horrors, have ensured that Madame Tussaud's remains one of London's most popular tourist attractions. (Map 3, K 17)*

As he looked round he suddenly saw for the first time the effigy in the window, and stood staring and pointing, too amazed for words.

"Tut! it's only a dummy," said the Count.

"A fake, is it? Well, strike me! Madame Tussaud ain't in it. It's the living spit of him, gown and all."

. . . "I've fooled better men than he," the Count answered. "The stone is here in my secret pocket. I take no chances leaving it about. It can be out of England to-night and cut into four pieces in Amsterdam before Sunday. He knows nothing of Van Seddar."

"I thought Van Seddar was going next week."

"He *was*. But now he must get off by the next boat. One or other of us must slip round with the stone to Lime Street and tell him."

"But the false bottom ain't ready."

"Well, he must take it as it is and chance it. There's not a moment to lose."

The address was "The Three Gables, Harrow Weald."

"So that's that!" said Holmes. "And now, if you can spare the time, Watson, we will get upon our way."

A short railway journey, and a shorter drive, brought us to the house, a brick and timber villa, standing in its own acre of undeveloped grassland. Three small projections above the upper windows made a feeble attempt to justify its name. Behind was a grove of melancholy, half-grown pines, and the whole aspect of the place was poor and depressing.

Left *The Holborn Bars are stone obelisks marking the boundary of the City of London at Holborn. One can be seen in the foreground of this photograph taken in 1885. To the right lie the Elizabethan buildings of Staple Inn. (Map 3, L 21)*

. . . "It was the killing of young Perkins outside the Holborn Bar—What! you're not going?"

The negro had sprung back, and his face was leaden. "I won't listen to no such talk," said he. "What have I to do with this 'ere Perkins, Masser Holmes? I was trainin' at the Bull Ring in Birmingham when this boy done gone get into trouble."

Left *Lime Street, c. 1890. This ancient street in the City is named after the purveyors of lime who once congregated here. (Map 3, M 23)*

Right *A scene in Harrow, North London in 1898. A gabled half-timbered building, typical to the area, can be seen in the distance.*

Left *A hansom cab stands outside Boodle's Club, St. James's Street, with its famous bow window. The photograph dates from 1907.*

Above *St. James's Street in 1900. This street has long been celebrated for its many clubs and luxury shops.* (*Map 3, M–N 18–19*)

. . . "Now, Watson, this is a case for Langdale Pike, and I am going to see him now. When I get back I may be clearer in the matter."

I saw no more of Holmes during the day, but I could well imagine how he spent it, for Langdale Pike was his human book of reference upon all matters of social scandal. This strange, languid creature spent his waking hours in the bow window of a St. James's Street club and was the receiving-station as well as the transmitter for all the gossip of the metropolis. He made, it was said, a four-figure income by the paragraphs which he contributed every week to the garbage papers which cater to an inquisitive public. If ever, far down in the turbid depths of London life, there was some strange swirl or eddy, it was marked with automatic exactness by this human dial upon the surface. Holmes discreetly helped Langdale to knowledge, and on occasion was helped in turn.

We had taken a cab and were speeding to some address in Grosvenor Square.

. . . It was one of the finest corner-houses of the West End. A machine-like footman took up our cards and returned with word that the lady was not at home. "Then we shall wait until she is," said Holmes cheerfully.

The machine broke down.

"Not at home means not at home to *you*," said the footman.

"Good," Holmes answered. "That means that we shall not have to wait. Kindly give this note to your mistress."

He scribbled three or four words upon a sheet of his notebook, folded it, and handed it to the man.

"What did you say, Holmes?" I asked.

"I simply wrote: 'Shall it be the police, then?' I think that should pass us in."

It did—with amazing celerity. A minute later we were in an Arabian Nights drawing-room, vast and wonderful, in a half gloom, picked out with an occasional pink electric light. The lady had come, I felt, to that time of life when even the proudest beauty finds the half light more welcome.

Above *A fine corner house in Grosvenor Square, c. 1914. (Map 3, M 17–18)*

Right *A Grosvenor Square drawing room in the early 1900s. For the very wealthy the opulent furnishings seen here were typical of the period.*

Holmes had read carefully a note which the last post had brought him. Then, with the dry chuckle which was his nearest approach to a laugh, he tossed it over to me.

Below *A house in Old Jewry, c. 1900. This street, and the surrounding area, was a Jewish ghetto until the nineteenth century. (Map 3 L–M 23)*

Right *Upper Baker Street Post Office in 1904. Post for Baker Street would have been sorted and delivered from here. (Map 3, K 17)*

"For a mixture of the modern and the mediæval, of the practical and of the wildly fanciful, I think this is surely the limit," said he. "What do you make of it, Watson?"

I read as follows:

46, OLD JEWRY
Nov. 19th

Re Vampires

SIR:

    Our client, Mr. Robert Ferguson, of Ferguson and Muirhead, tea brokers, of Mincing Lane, has made some inquiry from us in a communication of even date concerning vampires. As our firm specializes entirely upon the assessment of machinery the matter hardly comes within our purview, and we have therefore recommended Mr. Ferguson to call upon you and lay the matter before you. We have not forgotten your successful action in the case of Matilda Briggs.

We are, sir,
Faithfully yours,
MORRISON, MORRISON, AND DODD

It was twilight of a lovely spring evening, and even Little Ryder Street, one of the smaller offshoots from the Edgware Road, within a stone-cast of old Tyburn Tree of evil memory, looked golden and wonderful in the slanting rays of the setting sun. The particular house to which we were directed was a large, old-fashioned, Early Georgian edifice, with a flat brick face broken only by two deep bay windows on the ground floor. It was on this ground floor that our client lived, and, indeed, the low windows proved to be the front of the huge room in which he spent his waking hours.

Left *Waterloo Road in 1906.*
(*Map 3, N 21*)

Above *Edgware Road in 1897.*
(*Map 3, L 16*)

. . . "By the way, who is your house-agent?"

Our client was amazed at the sudden question.

"Holloway and Steele, in the Edgware Road. But why?"

"I am a bit of an archæologist myself when it comes to houses," said Holmes, laughing. "I was wondering if this was Queen Anne or Georgian."

"Georgian, beyond doubt."

. . . "'James Winter, alias Morecroft, alias Killer Evans,' was the inscription below." Holmes drew an envelope from his pocket. "I scribbled down a few points from his dossier: Aged forty-four. Native of Chicago. Known to have shot three men in the States. Escaped from penitentiary through political influence. Came to London in 1893. Shot a man over cards in a night-club in the Waterloo Road in January, 1895."

Our eyes fell upon a mass of rusted machinery, great rolls of paper, a litter of bottles, and, neatly arranged upon a small table, a number of neat little bundles.

"A printing press—a counterfeiter's outfit," said Holmes.

"Yes, sir," said our prisoner, staggering slowly to his feet and then sinking into the chair. "The greatest counterfeiter London ever saw. That's Prescott's machine, and those bundles on the table are two thousand of Prescott's notes worth a hundred each and fit to pass anywhere. Help yourselves, gentlemen. Call it a deal and let me beat it."

Holmes laughed.

"We don't do things like that, Mr. Evans. There is no bolt-hole for you in this country. You shot this man Prescott, did you not?"

"Yes, sir, and got five years for it, though it was he who pulled on me. Five years—when I should have had a medal the size of a soup plate. No living man could tell a Prescott from a Bank of England, and if I hadn't put him out he would have flooded London with them. I was the only one in the world who knew where he made them."

The letter which he handed to me, written in a bold, masterful hand, ran as follows:

CLARIDGE'S HOTEL
October 3rd

DEAR MR. SHERLOCK HOLMES,

I can't see the best woman God ever made go to her death without doing all that is possible to save her. I can't explain things—I can't even try to explain them, but I know beyond all doubt that Miss Dunbar is innocent. You know the facts—who doesn't? . . .

Somewhere in the vaults of the bank of Cox and Co., at Charing Cross, there is a travel-worn and battered tin dispatch-box with my name, John H. Watson, M.D., Late Indian Army, painted upon the lid. It is crammed with papers, nearly all of which are records of cases to illustrate the curious problems which Mr. Sherlock Holmes had at various times to examine.

Left *The Bank of England, Threadneedle Street in 1895. Established in 1694, the building was reconstructed in the late 1780s by the fine Georgian architect John Soane and underwent less attractive modifications in the 1920s and 1930s. (Map 3, M 23)*

Above *Cox and King's Bank ('Cox & Co.') in Craig's Court, Charing Cross is the porticoed building on the right in this photograph, which dates from the early 1900s. (Map 3, N 20)*

Right *An interior view of Claridge's Hotel, Brook Street, in 1910. (Map 3, M 18)*

The Adventure of the Creeping Man

Holmes stopped at a post-office and sent off a telegram on our way. The answer reached us in the evening, and he tossed it across to me.

HAVE VISITED THE COMMERCIAL ROAD AND SEEN DORAK. SUAVE PERSON, BOHEMIAN, ELDERLY. KEEPS LARGE GENERAL STORE.

MERCER.

Left A traffic accident in the Commercial Road in 1890. This important thoroughfare was built in the early nineteenth century to improve transport between the newly constructed East and West India Docks and the City. (Map 4, L–M 25–26)

Right Curzon Street in the 1890s. This fashionable street was laid out in the eighteenth century and attracted many famous residents, including Benjamin Disraeli who died here in 1881. The building in the right of the photograph is the Mayfair Chapel, which was demolished in 1899. (Map 3, N 18)

The Adventure of the Veiled Lodger

One forenoon—it was late in 1896—I received a hurried note from Holmes asking for my attendance. When I arrived I found him seated in a smoke-laden atmosphere, with an elderly, motherly woman of the buxom landlady type in the corresponding chair in front of him.

"This is Mrs. Merrilow, of South Brixton," said my friend with a wave of the hand. "Mrs. Merrilow does not object to tobacco, Watson, if you wish to indulge your filthy habits. Mrs. Merrilow has an interesting story to tell which may well lead to further developments in which your presence may be useful"

Right South Brixton in 1898. By the late nineteenth century Brixton had become a popular middle-class suburb. (Map 2, T 20–21)

. . . "By the way, Watson, you know something of racing?"

"I ought to. I pay for it with about half my wound pension."

"Then I'll make you my 'Handy Guide to the Turf.' What about Sir Robert Norberton? Does the name recall anything?"

"Well, I should say so. He lives at Shoscombe Old Place, and I know it well, for my summer quarters were down there

once. Norberton nearly came within your province once."

"How was that?"

"It was when he horsewhipped Sam Brewer, the well-known Curzon Street money-lender, on Newmarket Heath. He nearly killed the man."

"Ah, he sounds interesting! Does he often indulge in that way?"

"Well, he has the name of being a dangerous man.

. . . "On that particular evening old Amberley, wishing to give his wife a treat, had taken two upper circle seats at the Haymarket Theatre. At the last moment she had complained of a headache and had refused to go. He had gone alone. There seemed to be no doubt about the fact, for he produced the unused ticket which he had taken for his wife."

"That is remarkable—most remarkable," said Holmes, whose interest in the case seemed to be rising. "Pray continue, Watson. I find your narrative most arresting. Did you personally examine this ticket? You did not, perchance, take the number?"

"It so happens that I did," I answered with some pride. "It chanced to be my old school number, thirty-one, and so is stuck in my head."

"Excellent, Watson! His seat, then, was either thirty or thirty-two."

"Quite so," I answered with some mystification. "And on B row."

Left *The exterior of the Theatre Royal, Haymarket, in 1895. Founded in 1720, the current structure dates from 1821 and was built by John Nash. Between 1887 and 1896 the distinguished manager Beerbohm Tree steered the Haymarket to many theatrical successes, including first productions of Oscar Wilde's* A Woman of No Importance *in 1893, and* An Ideal Husband *in 1895. (Map 3, M 19)*

Opposite *An audience at the Theatre Royal, Haymarket in 1899.*

. . . "Let us escape from this weary workaday world by the side door of music. Carina sings to-night at the Albert Hall, and we still have time to dress, dine, and enjoy."

Above *The Albert Hall, South Kensington, in 1890. Completed in 1871 by Major-General H.G.D. Scott to the designs of Captain Fowke, it was built as a memorial to Prince Albert (1819–61), Queen Victoria's husband. (Map 3, N 15)*

An
Atlas of Victorian London

G. W. Bacon published the maps reproduced here in 1888. His New Large-Scale Ordnance Map of London & Suburbs *was made up of four inch and nine inch maps and unrivalled in the quality of detail and extent of the Capital shown.*

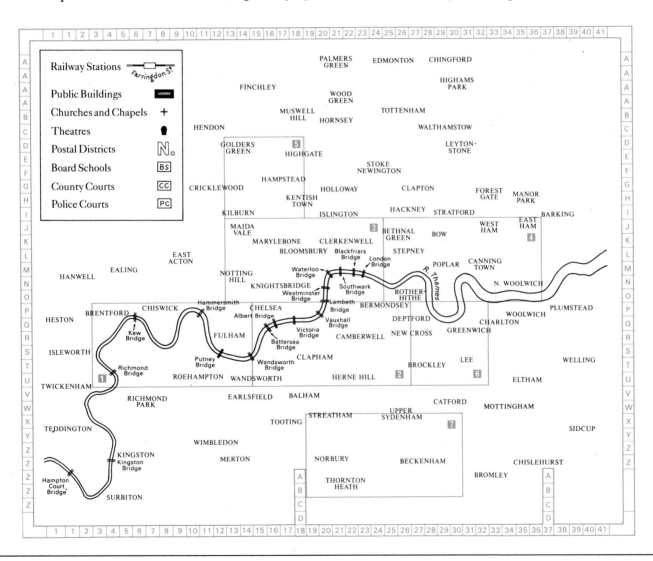

MAP 5

MAP 6

P

Q

R

S

T

U

MAP 7

Acknowledgments

This book would not have been possible without access to the following excellent photographic libraries and museums: the London Borough of Camden Local History Libraries, the Guildhall Library, the Greater London Photograph Library, the Royal Borough of Kensington and Chelsea Libraries, the London Transport Museum, the London Borough of Lambeth Archives Department, Bromley Public Libraries, Croydon Public Libraries, the Museum of London, the Metropolitan Police Historical Museum, the National Railway Museum, the Royal Commission on the Historical Monuments of England, the British Architectural Library, RIBA, London, and Westminster City Libraries.

In addition I would like to thank the following for their help in locating various photographs: the Department of Medical Illustration at St. Bartholomew's Hospital, Lloyds Bank Archives Department, Douglas Schatz and Ken Brown of Stanford's, and the Savoy Hotels. Thanks are also due to Michael Cox, Andrew Robinson and Lesley Beames of Granada for their kind permission to reproduce a still from the recent Sherlock Holmes television series.

The London Encyclopaedia by Ben Weinreb and Christopher Hibbert (Macmillan, 1983) has been an invaluable source of information when compiling this book. Contemporary maps of the metropolis from *The A–Z of Victorian London* (Margary, Guildhall 1987) have been extensively featured, and I am grateful to the publisher for permission to reproduce them. I am obliged to Martin Soames who kindly traced a copy of the informative guide book *London in 1889.*

Finally, I am indebted to Chris Denvir of the Greater London Photograph Library for his tireless help in locating a range of photographs; Catherine Cooke, Systems Librarian at the Westminster City Libraries, for her extensive knowledge of Holmesiana; Phoebe Phillips and Tim Probart for their enthusiasm and encouragement; and Rachael Foster for her inspired design work.

Picture Credits

(b = bottom; bl = bottom left; br = bottom right; t = top; tl = top left; tr = top right; r = right; l = left)

BBC Hulton Picture Library 95, 108l, 109bl, 118, 127br, 153; *The British Architectural Library, RIBA, London* 87; *Bromley Public Libraries* 82b, 117bl; *London Borough of Camden Local History Library* 11r, 16tr, 51bl, 90, 143tl; *London Borough of Croydon Public Library* 83br, 119; *Granada TV* 2; *Greater London Photograph Library* 9br, 14, 15, 20, 22tr, 25, 26l, 29, 35, 36, 38t, 39, 41, 44t, 45, 47t, 50tr, 51t, 52bl, 53bl, 54, 55tl, 57, 59br, 60bl, 66, 67, 72bl, 75, 77br, 79bl, 82tr, 89, 91, 94tr, 98, 99br, 101bl, 103t, 107bl, 110, 116bl, 117tr, 121br, 122tr, 123, 125tr, 126, 127bl, 135, 137tl, 143br, 148, 149tl, 150tl, 152, 154; *Guildhall Library, City of London* 11tl, 17, 40br, 43t, 47br, 52tr, 56tl, 62tl, 71tr, 99tl, 103bl, 105, 116tr, 130tr, 139br, 140, 144tr, 145tl, 146bl; *Hunting Aerofilms* 31br; *Royal Borough of Kensington and Chelsea Libraries and Arts Service* 37, 80, 93, 113tr, 124tr; *London Borough of Lambeth Archives Department* 129, 150br; *Lloyds Bank Archives Department* 88; *London Transport Museum* 26tr, 122bl, 141, 147tr; *Mansell Collection* 137br; *Metropolitan Police Historical Museum* 62br, 121tl; *Museum of London* 31, 34, 50l, 115; *National Railway Museum Photographic Collection* 97b; *Royal Commission on the Historical Monuments of England* 10, 13, 21r, 22bl, 23, 24, 27, 28, 30t, 33br, 43br, 44bl, 46, 48, 49, 53t, 55br, 59t, 61, 63, 64br, 68, 69, 70, 71bl, 72tr, 73, 74, 76, 79tr, 81, 85, 92, 96, 100, 101tr, 102, 106, 107r, 111, 124b, 125bl, 128, 130bl, 131, 136, 139t, 142, 144l, 147bl, 151; *The Savoy Hotel PLC* 149br; *St Bartholomew's Hospital* 12; *The Victoria and Albert Museum* 42; *Westminster City Archives* 6, 9tl, 19, 21l, 33tl, 38br, 40tl, 56br, 60tr, 64tl, 65br, 77tl, 112br, 113bl, 133, 134, 146tr.